THE ENCYCLOPEDIA OF
HOMEMADE
PRESERVES

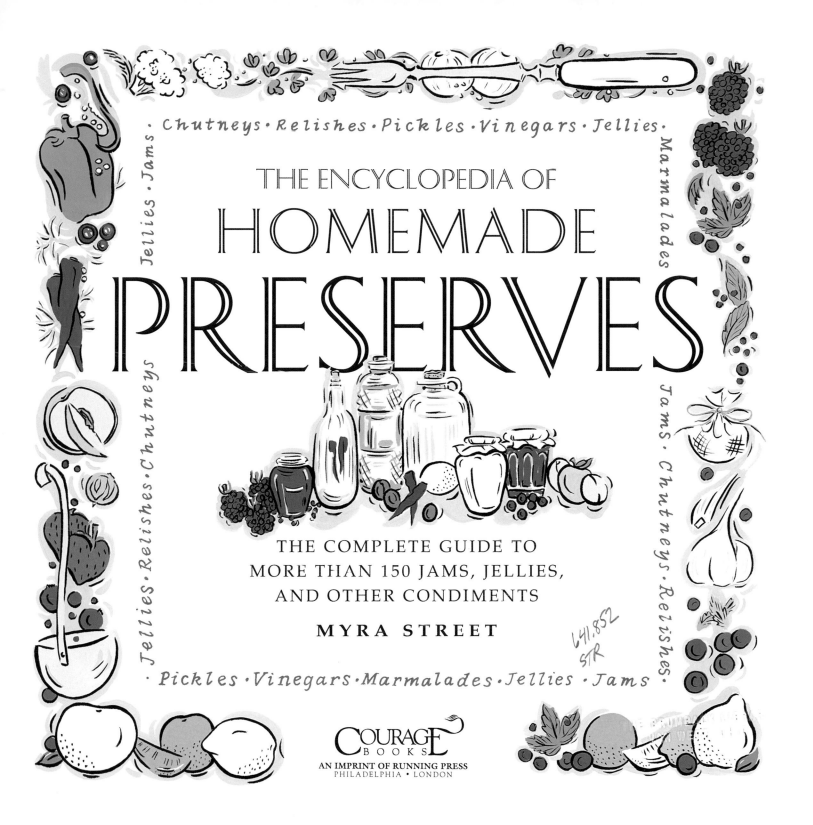

Chutneys · Relishes · Pickles · Vinegars · Jellies ·

Jellies · Jams · Marmalades

THE ENCYCLOPEDIA OF
HOMEMADE
PRESERVES

Jellies · Relishes · Chutneys

Jams · Chutneys · Relishes

THE COMPLETE GUIDE TO
MORE THAN 150 JAMS, JELLIES,
AND OTHER CONDIMENTS

MYRA STREET

641.852
STR

· Pickles · Vinegars · Marmalades · Jellies · Jams ·

COURAGE
BOOKS

AN IMPRINT OF RUNNING PRESS
PHILADELPHIA · LONDON

A QUINTET BOOK

9 8 7 6 5 4 3 2 1

Digit on the right indicates the number of
this printing

Library of Congress
Cataloging-in-Publication Number 95–70142

ISBN 1–56138–571–9

This book was designed and produced by
Quintet Publishing Limited
6 Blundell Street
London N7 9BH

Creative Director: Richard Dewing
Designer: Ian Hunt
Senior Editor: Laura Sandelson
Editor: Caroline Ball
Illustrator: Joanne Makin

Typeset in Great Britain by
Central Southern Typesetters, Eastbourne
Manufactured in Singapore by
Eray Scan (Pte) Ltd.
Printed in Singapore by
Star Standard Industries (Pte) Ltd.

Published by Courage Books
an imprint of Running Press Book Publishers
125 South Twenty-second Street
Philadelphia, Pennsylvania 19103–4399

12.85

Contents

TO THE READER OR COOK:

This volume includes some recipes for making your own flavored oils. Please be advised that researchers at the FDA's Center for Food Safety and Applied Nutrition have raised concerns about potential health hazards caused when bacteria existing in the flavoring items are introduced to the airless environment of the oil. To prevent any illness or side effects, we recommend the following steps:

• Heat crushed garlic and herbs in olive oil to release flavors, rather than using the infusion technique.

• Keep flavored oils refrigerated. Make small batches and use within 12 to 24 hours.

• Add vinegar to your oil. Its high acidity reduces the potential for bacteria to grow.

Introduction
~

THE WIDE SCOPE of preserving foods in season stretches way beyond the cozy picture of the farmhouse pantry and the artistically labeled jars of jam and pickles. Centuries of skill in preserving food before the advent of freezing have given us a wonderful heritage to draw from. In this busy and high-tech age, it is interesting to see that commercially prepared jams, jellies, and pickles, although of a reasonable standard, are rarely in the same class as the homemade variety.

The main objective of food preservation is to use the food at maximum palatability and nutritive value, before the natural decaying process begins. Most people who are interested in preserving food use freezers and refrigerators, and these are now the main ways of storing food in good condition. Indeed, the freezer can be an invaluable aid to making homemade preserves because the fruit can be stored in the freezer until time is available to prepare and cook it. In this way, home preserves can be made in small batches to benefit many people who work outside the home and are unable to spend hours over the stove when the fruit is just ripe or the Seville oranges are in season.

We now have the advantage of buying many fruits and vegetables out of season since they are brought in from all parts of the world. This type of produce is usually expensive, and it is still better to preserve fruit and vegetables in season for flavor and quality. Raspberries, strawberries, plums, cherries, and blackberries all make delicious jams, but the end product would be too expensive if imported fruit were used.

Although the cost of ingredients and fuel has now increased, it is still possible to save money and eat delicious home preserves if you are willing to take the time. People with compact kitchens and little storage space can make small quantities and will find the microwave oven useful for producing a regular supply of homemade jam or marmalade.

Many people are experimenting with home-preserving for the first time, not only to obtain excellent flavors but to ensure the ingredients are fresh, wholesome, and free from artificial preservatives.

Homemade jams, jellies, and marmalades should be eaten within a year for maximum flavor because chemical substances called enzymes are naturally introduced into the food during the home preservation process and will eventually break down and produce molds and bacteria which will cause the food to deteriorate. This is why you may have had to scrape the mold from a precious jar of jam. This usually means that it has been kept too long, been badly sealed, or been stored in a damp place. It is quite safe to eat jam when mold has been removed. All homemade preserves should be rotated and eaten before the fruits and vegetables come into season the next year.

Equipment for simple home-preserving is minimal, and although a large preserving pan is useful if you intend to make jams and marmalade several times a year, a large, thick-bottomed, everyday saucepan can also be used. Glass jars must be thoroughly washed and sterilized to prevent jams, jellies, pickles, and chutneys from spoiling. Fill the jars right to the top and cover with waxed discs while hot. Alternatively, seal with metal lids and screw bands, as described on page 9.

Making flavored oils and vinegars is also simple and effective, and can add extra taste when making salad dressings, as well as when cooking meats, vegetables, and fish.

Some of the recipes in this book yield large quantities. Perhaps more than you care to make. If so, the amounts of ingredients needed in each recipe may simply be halved to give a smaller yield.

CHAPTER ONE

Jams for
Every Season

~

PRESERVING FRUIT IN jam is one of the more satisfying cooking tasks because the finished products are pretty, colorful jars of jam to enjoy throughout the year, unlike a cake or dessert which is quickly eaten.

Making jams, jellies, and marmalades is still the most popular form of fruit preservation today. Once you have tasted really good homemade preserves, you will always want to eat them. People who grow fruit in the garden often have too much to eat at one time and even to store in the freezer; therefore, the surplus is ideal for jam. Those of us who do not have gardens capable of growing fruit can also make jam if we keep an eye on prices when the soft fruits are in season. There is usually a time when prices in supermarkets are low enough to make jam viable. There are also now many pick-your-own fruit farms and these are well worth a day in the country with the family or friends to make sure you have a supply of jam for the rest of the year. Do take your own containers because the fruit growers often charge for them.

What makes a good jam?

All jams and marmalades are preserves of cooked fruit boiled with sugar until setting or "jell" point is reached. A well-made jam has a bright color with the full flavor of the fruit, and should set or jell without becoming too stiff. In some jams, such as strawberry and cherry, the color and flavor are more important than the jell.

The shelf life of jam depends on the proportion of sugar to fruit, and jam must contain at least 65% sugar if it is to be kept for any length of time. Sugar is therefore a very important preserving agent in jams, jellies, and marmalades; it has an influence on the flavor and reacts with the pectin and acid to obtain a good jell.

A good jam, jelly, or marmalade should be well jelled without being stiff. The end product should have a good flavor, a clear bright color, and good shelf life. Jams and marmalades should keep in good condition for well over one year. It is best to use up jam at this stage and make new jam with the next year's fruits. Some color and flavor will be lost and the jam may dry up if it is keep too long, even under the best storage conditions.

EQUIPMENT FOR JAM-MAKING

A PRESERVING PAN, such as a Dutch oven or cast-iron kettle, is useful if you intend to make jams or chutneys regularly; otherwise, use a very large saucepan with a thick bottom. Old copper and brass preserving pans are best kept for decoration because they react with the vitamin C in the fruit. If used, they must be scrupulously clean because verdigris can form in these old pans.

It is best to cook hard fruit in a saucepan with a lid before making jam because the wide preserving pan allows too much evaporation.

Rub butter around the preserving pan before making jam to prevent sticking and reduce foam.

A WOODEN SPOON is needed with a handle long enough to ensure it does not fall into the large pan.

JARS should only be used if they are undamaged. Wash thoroughly with detergent, and then rinse several times with hot water. Do not dry with a cloth, but shake out excess water and dry in the oven.

MASON JARS have special metal lids and screw bands for sealing that can be used instead of waxed discs or paraffin. Use sterilized jars and lids, and fill, allowing ½-inch headspace. Place the flat lid on the jar with the sealing compound on the rim, then screw on the band tightly. If liked, the jars can be processed in a water-bath, following the directions of a canning manual.

JAM COVERS should be waxed discs to fit the jars, with cellophane tops which are fastened by rubber bands. Once the jam is covered with a waxed disc, the jar can then be covered with a clean cloth or piece of parchment paper until the jam is cool. The jars can then be covered with stretched plastic wrap. Do not use commercial metal screw tops because the jam will go moldy.

A WIDEMOUTHED PLASTIC FUNNEL saves messy jar filling. Place the funnel in the jar, and scoop out the jam with a ladle or jug. Use a saucer under the jug to avoid spills.

A CANDY THERMOMETER is not essential, but is a great help if you intend on making lots of jams and marmalades. How to use one is discussed in testing jam (see page 10).

LABELS should be written with the type of jam and the date the jam was made.

JELLYING JAMS AND JELLIES

The set or jell, which allows the jam to be spread, is dependent on a gum-like substance called pectin that is found in the fruit. The pectin reacts with the acid and sugar to form a jell.

In ripe fruit, the pectin is soluble and can be set free easily by stewing or crushing the fruit for a short time. Under-ripe fruit has an insoluble form of pectin known as pectose (also present in citrus fruits which explains the long cooking when making marmalade), and this can be converted to pectin by simmering with acid (lemon juice or tartaric acid). Over-ripe fruit contains pectic acid which is useless for jam making, so **do not use over-ripe fruit to make jam**.

GUIDE TO THE PECTIN CONTENT OF FRUITS USED FOR JAM- AND JELLY-MAKING		
HIGH	**MEDIUM**	**LOW**
Crabapples	Dessert apples	Bananas
Cranberries	Apricots	Cherries
Cooking apples	Blackberries	Figs
Black currants	Greengage plums	Grapes
Elderberries	Loganberries	Vegetable marrows
Red currants	Mulberries	Melons
Damson plums	Plums	Nectarines
Gooseberries	Raspberries	Peaches
Lemons		Pineapple
Limes		Strawberries
Seville oranges		Rhubarb
Quinces		
Plums (some)		

Of the three ingredients needed to form a jell, sugar is the only one that can be added in exact quantities. The amount of the other two depends on the state of the fruit.

Acid is often added in the form of lemon juice because it helps the pectin to form a jell, prevents crystals of sugar from forming during storage, and improves the color and flavor of the jam.

Fruits contain different amounts of pectin, and some make the jam-making process simple because they are high in the substance. Often two fruits, such as blackberry and apple, are combined to make a pectin-strong mixture.

Fruit with a high pectin content requires some water in the cooking process to prevent the jam from becoming too stiff.

Only a small amount of water is added to the hard fruits in the Medium column to soften them and free the pectin, and this will be boiled away before the addition of sugar.

No water is added to the Low group, but acid (lemon juice or tartaric acid) is added, as well as some other fruit which is high in pectin, such as cooking apples or red currants.

Adding acid

It is essential to add acid to low-pectin fruits to produce a jell. Add 2 tbsp lemon juice or ½–1 tsp tartaric acid (available from supermarkets) to 2¼ lb fruit. Add the acid to the fruit before cooking, except if using dried fruit.

A fruit with little pectin can be combined with one with a high pectin content for a better flavor and jell. Red currant, gooseberry juice, and apples are often used in this way, for example:

- strawberry with red currant
- cherry with red currant or gooseberry
- blackberry and apple
- pear and apple

Commercially prepared pectin

This can be bought in the supermarket for use with low pectin fruit. If using, follow the instructions carefully. The combination fruits will work equally well.

SUGAR IN JAM-MAKING

Sugar is an important ingredient in jam-making because it is the substance which preserves the fruit and gives it a good shelf life. Too much or too little sugar will result in a poor jell, and the flavoring of the jam will be spoiled by too much sugar.

Homemade jams which combine the best combinations of shelf life, a good jell, and excellent flavor and color are obtained when 60% of the final weight of the jam is provided by the added sugar. For each 6 lb sugar, a yield of about 5 qts jam is possible.

Suitable sugar for jams and jellies

Both cane and beet sugar are suitable for preserving.

GRANULATED SUGAR is the cheapest and most widely used sugar. It is suited to preserving, provided it is given sufficient time to dissolve completely. Many people make excellent preserves with it.

GRANULATED BROWN SUGAR is a natural beet sugar which is suitable for jams and jellies.

PRESERVING SUGAR is a sugar with large crystals, ideally suited to making jams and jellies. The crystals dissolve slowly and retain enough space between them to prevent the sugar settling in a dense layer at the bottom of the pan. This prevents any sticking, and the jam requires less attention. Preserving sugar produces less froth and foam, which means the preserves require less skimming and the jam should be brighter.

JAM SUGAR is a special sugar for making jam and is especially suitable for use with low pectin fruit, such as strawberries and cherries. It is excellent for beginners making a small quantity of jam, but it is more expensive for large quantities.

LIGHT BROWN SUGAR can be used in some marmalades and jams to give a rich color. It is also useful in chutneys.

DARK BROWN SUGAR is suitable for chutneys and pickles.

MOLASSES SUGAR contains the highest amount of natural molasses and is almost black in color. Use in recipes which call for dark brown sugar, such as fruitcakes, mincemeat, and some chutneys and pickles.

DEMERARA SUGAR has large sparkling crystals with a crunchy, sticky texture and a rich aroma. It is used for coffee and crumb toppings on cakes and desserts, and only used in preserving in special recipes.

TURBINADO SUGAR is similar to demerara and can be used in the same way.

SUPERFINE SUGAR is light and has a fine grain. It is more expensive than granulated and is only used in preserving in special recipes.

In most recipes, it is suggested that the sugar is warmed. This is not essential, but it does help the sugar to dissolve more quickly when added to the hot fruit. Heat the sugar in the oven with the jam jars, making sure that it is in an ovenproof container. The sugar is then dissolved over a low heat, stirring from time to time.

Sugar has a hardening effect on fruits such as black currants and damsons, therefore it is essential to soften the fruit thoroughly before adding the sugar.

TESTING THE JAM FOR JELLYING

Although it is quite easy to make jams and jellies with simple household tests, anyone who makes a great deal of jam or marmalade will find that investing in a candy thermometer is the best way to test for the jell point.

To use a candy thermometer for jam, it should first be put into hot water. Stir the jam thoroughly before the temperature is tested, and take the thermometer straight from the hot water to the hot jam. The bulb of the thermometer should not rest on the bottom of the pan. The temperature for jam or jelly should be about 220°F. At the same time, it is useful to do the cold plate test.

Cold plate test

Put a plate in the freezer or freezing compartment of the refrigerator for five minutes. Place a scant teaspoon of the jam on the plate. If the jam has reached jell point, the surface should jell and become crinkly. Use only a small amount of jam, or it will not cool down quickly enough to give a true test.

The flake test

Dip a wooden spoon into the jam and turn it horizontally in the hand until the jam on it is slightly cooled. The jam will run off the edge in large flakes, instead of droplets, if the jam is jelled.

CANNING AND STORING JAM

Clean glass jars can be placed on newspapers on the oven shelves in a low oven, ready for the jam. Remove any foam from the jam at this stage; constant skimming during cooking is not necessary and will reduce the yield. Lift the hot jars onto a heatproof surface and place the preserving pan beside them. Pour the hot jam into the jars using a jug or ladle, preferably through a wide plastic funnel stuck in the mouth of the jar (this will stop any drips).

Sparkling Strawberry Jam

The favorite summer fruits do make the most delicious jams. A scone with homemade jam, especially strawberry or raspberry, makes a special treat for an afternoon tea. You may have to find a hiding place for your jam if you have a family because it can disappear quite rapidly. Beware of overboiling these delicate jams, since the color and texture can be impaired.

MAKES 5 QT

7 lb strawberries, hulled
juice of 2 lemons
6 lb sugar, warmed

Wash the strawberries, if necessary, and pat dry with some paper towels. Put in the preserving pan with the lemon juice. Stir gently over a low heat to produce some juice and reduce the volume of the fruit.

Add the sugar and stir over a low heat, from time to time, until the sugar is completely dissolved. Bring the jam to a rolling boil for a few minutes, then test for jellying or allow the candy thermometer to reach 220°F.

Remove any foam which has formed, and allow the jam to cool until a skin is just forming. This will make sure that the fruit does not float to the top of the jars. Pour into hot jars, seal, cover, and label.

Microwave Strawberry Jam

MAKES ABOUT 6 CUPS

2 lb strawberries, hulled
3 tbsp lemon juice
4½ cups sugar

Rinse the strawberries and pat dry with paper towels. Put into a large (7½-pt) bowl suitable for the microwave.

Add the sugar, mix well, then microwave on high for 5 minutes. Remove and stir well to dissolve the sugar.

Return to the microwave oven and cook for 10–12 minutes on high, stirring twice during the cooking time. Remove from the oven, skim off any foam, and test for jellying.

Allow to stand for a few minutes. Pour into hot jars, seal, cover, and label.

Freezer Jam

This is more a conserve than a jam, and it can be served semi-frozen. Raspberries, strawberries, peaches, and nectarines are all suitable. For peaches and nectarines, there is no need to skin, just pit and mince in the food processor or chop finely with a knife.

MAKES ABOUT 4 CUPS

1 lb fresh soft fruit
2 cups sugar
2 tbsp lemon juice

Place the prepared fruit in a large bowl with the sugar and the lemon juice. Stir and leave in a warm place for several hours, or until the fruit has softened and the sugar dissolved.

Pour into small plastic containers and freeze with a dated label. The jam can be frozen for 9 months, but once opened, it can only be stored in the refrigerator for 3 weeks.

The jam will need about 15–20 minutes to defrost.

Dazzling Raspberry Jam

This is one of the most delicious and favorite jams; it should be a brilliant jewel color with a fresh flavor. It is best made with fruit which is just ripe. As it is important to gauge the boiling temperature, it is made more accurately with a candy thermometer.

MAKES 7 PTS

4 lb raspberries
2 tbsp lemon juice
4 lb sugar, warmed

Heat the washed fruit and lemon juice gently in the pan until the juice starts to flow. Add the sugar and stir, from time to time, over a low heat until completely dissolved. Bring to a rolling boil and test after 3 minutes or, using the candy thermometer, when the temperature reaches 220°F. Try not to overboil because the flavor and color will spoil.

Pour into hot jars, seal, cover, and label.

Microwave Raspberry Jam

MAKES 6 CUPS

2 lb raspberries
3 tbsp lemon juice
4½ cups sugar

If using frozen raspberries, defrost them for about 8 minutes, or cook for 3 minutes if using fresh. Add the lemon juice and allow the fruit to cook for a further 2 minutes.

Stir in the sugar and cook at full power for 4 minutes. Remove from the oven and stir.

Cook on high for about 15–20 minutes, but stir after 10 minutes and again after a further 5 minutes. Test for jellying, but this jam always jells well after cooling so do not be too alarmed if it seems a little runny.

Allow to cool slightly since it is very hot to handle. Pour into hot jars, seal, cover, and label.

Speedy Microwave Raspberry Jam

MAKES 3 CUPS

1 lb frozen raspberries
2 tbsp lemon juice
2 cups granulated or preserving sugar

Put the raspberries in a large bowl suitable for the microwave oven. Allow to defrost for 3 minutes, then cook for 2 minutes on high.

Add lemon juice, stir in the sugar, and cook on high for 4 minutes. Stir thoroughly. Cook for a further 15 minutes, remove any foam, and allow to stand for 3 minutes.

Pour into hot jars, seal, cover, and label.

Uncooked Raspberry Jam

MAKES 4 CUPS

1 lb raspberries
2½ cups sugar

The raspberries must be firm, ripe, and dry, or the jam will not keep. To clean, roll gently in paper towels. Put in a bowl with the sugar, and beat well until the sugar is completely dissolved; this can take 30–40 minutes. Alternatively, use an electric mixer or a food processor for a shorter preparation time. When the sugar is dissolved, pour into jars, cover, and store in the refrigerator, or the freezer if keeping for any time. Eat within two weeks.

Ruby Rhubarb and Raspberry Jam

MAKES ABOUT 7 CUPS

1½ lb rhubarb
11 oz raspberries (frozen can be used)
juice of 1 lemon
4½ cups sugar, warmed

Wash the rhubarb and raspberries. Cut the rhubarb into small pieces. Put both fruits with the lemon juice into a large pan. Stir over a low heat until juice starts to run from the raspberries. Allow to simmer for a few minutes (do not burn), and then add the sugar.

Continue cooking over a low heat, stirring from time to time until the sugar is dissolved and the rhubarb is soft.

Bring to a rolling boil for about 4 minutes, and then test for jellying or use the candy thermometer until it reads 220°F.

Pour into hot jars, seal, cover, and label.

Jeweled Raspberry and Red Currant Jam

The combination of red currants and raspberries gives the jam a superb flavor and a brilliant color. .

MAKES ABOUT 5 QT

2½ cups red currant juice (see below)
4 lb raspberries
6 lb preserving sugar, warmed
2 tbsp lemon juice

Make the red currant juice by simmering 2¼ lb red currants in the microwave until soft (about 10 minutes), or in a saucepan with 1 tbsp water. When soft, liquidize and strain through a nylon sieve.

Put the raspberries into a pan and allow them to warm over a low heat. When the juice starts to run, add the red currant juice, lemon juice, and stir gently. Allow the fruit to simmer gently for about 20 minutes.

Add the warmed sugar and stir until it is completely dissolved. Bring the jam to a rolling boil, and after 3–5 minutes, test for jellying, or use the candy thermometer until it reaches 220°F.

Pour into hot jars, seal, cover, and label.

Raspberry and Apple Jam

MAKES 4 QT

2¼ lb cooking apples, peeled, cored and sliced
juice of 2 lemons
⅔ cup water
2¼ lb raspberries, hulled, washed and drained
4 lb preserving sugar, warmed

Place the apples in a pan, mix, and stir in the sugar with the lemon juice and water. Simmer until tender for about 15 minutes.

Add the raspberries, sprinkle on the warmed sugar, and simmer gently until the sugar is completely dissolved. Bring to a boil for about 5 minutes. Test for setting, or use the candy thermometer to 220°F.

Allow to stand for 2–3 minutes, remove any foam, and pour into hot jars. Seal, cover, and label.

Cherry and Red Currant Jam

MAKES 5 QT

1½ cups red currant juice (see below)
6 lb Morello cherries
6 lb sugar, warmed

You will need about 1½ lb red currants to make the juice. Put the washed currants in the microwave for 8 minutes until the juice runs, or in a small saucepan over a very low heat. Mash the fruit with a potato masher, or put through a liquidizer or food processor. Rub through a coarse sieve until you have 1½ cups of juice.

Remove the pits from the cherries, preferably with a cherry pitter, over a bowl to catch the juice. If you prefer, put them in a pan with ⅔ cup water and stew for about 10 minutes until soft, then transfer the cherries to a bowl. Allow to cool, then remove the pits. Crack about 20 cherry pits, remove the kernels, and tie into a cheesecloth bag.

Put the red currant juice into the preserving pan with the sugar, and allow the sugar to dissolve over a low heat. When the sugar is completely dissolved, add the cherries and bring to a rolling boil for about 10–15 minutes. Test for jellying or use the candy thermometer which should reach 220°F.

Pour into hot jars, seal, cover, and label.

Luscious Cherry Jam

Cherries have practically no pectin, therefore it is a more difficult jam to make. It is possible to obtain a good jell by using a high proportion of sugar to fruit. Cut the acid in half if using Morello cherries. The black sweet cherries are more suitable for canning or freezing whole.

MAKES ABOUT 6 QT

10 lb cherries, weight after removing pits
juice of 5 lemons or ½ oz citric or tartaric acid
7 lb sugar, warmed

After pitting the cherries with a pitter, place the pits on a square of cheesecloth with the peel of at least one lemon, cut up. Tie the cheesecloth into a bag, and place in the preserving pan with the cherries, lemon juice, and ⅔ cup water. Heat slowly over a low heat until the juice runs, then simmer until the cherries are tender, which will take about 30 minutes.

Add the warmed sugar and stir until completely dissolved. Bring the pan to a rolling boil until the jam reaches jellying point, or the candy thermometer reaches 220°F. Allow to stand for a few minutes and remove any foam from the surface.

Pour into hot jars, seal, cover, and label.

Fragrant Rose Petal Jam

MAKES ABOUT 5 CUPS

1 lb rose petals
1 lb lemons
2 cups sugar, warmed

Trim off the white tips of the rose petals. Slice the lemons very thinly with a sharp knife, put in a saucepan, and just cover with water. Bring to a boil, then drain, retaining the liquid.

Add the sugar to the lemons and stir until dissolved with 2 tbsp of the drained liquid. Stir in the rose petals, and cook until the mixture is thick. Pour into hot jars, seal, cover, and label.

Black Currant Jam

Black currants are sometimes scarce now, but can often be found in specialty produce markets in season, during the months of July and August.

MAKES 5 PT

2¼ lb blackcurrants
4 cups water
3 lb sugar, warmed

Remove stems and trim the black currants, then wash in a colander. Put them into a medium-sized pan, cover with the measured water, and cover with a lid. A good depth of fruit and water is necessary to avoid too much moisture loss.

Stew the black currants until the skins are very soft. This may take 20–30 minutes, but do make sure they are tender. Transfer to a preserving or larger pan. Add the warmed sugar and stir until it is completely dissolved. Bring the black currants to a rolling boil and test for jellying after about 10–15 minutes, or wait until the candy thermometer reaches 220°F.

Pour into hot jars, seal, cover, and label.

Queen Claude's Breakfast Jam

In France greengage plums are called Queen Claude's plums because they were a favorite of hers.

MAKES 5 PT

3 lb greengages, halved and pitted
1¼ cups water
2 tbsp lemon juice
3 lb sugar, warmed

Crack some of the pits and remove the kernels. Place them on a square of cheesecloth and tie into a bag. Put the fruit with the water and lemon juice in a large saucepan and stew until tender, but not mushed. You will need another 1¼ cups water if the fruit is under-ripe.

Transfer to the preserving pan, remove the cheesecloth bag, and squeeze to make sure all the juice goes into the jam.

Add the sugar, stir well over a low heat, then allow to dissolve slowly, stirring from time to time. When the sugar is dissolved, bring the pan to a boil, and stir from time to time to prevent sticking. Boil for 5 minutes and test for jellying, or wait until the candy thermometer reaches 220°F.

Pour into hot jars, seal, cover, and label.

Damson Jam

MAKES 5 PT

4½ lb damson plums, washed and pitted
2½ cups water
5 lb sugar, warmed

Put the damsons in a large ovenproof casserole dish, pour on the water, and cover with a tight lid. Place in an oven preheated to 300°F for several hours, or until the fruit is tender and the juice has run out. This step can also be done in a microwave oven by putting a bowl in at high for 15 minutes; stir and allow to stand for 5 minutes. Repeat this procedure three times.

Remove damsons from the oven, and measure the fruit and liquid into the preserving pan. Add an equal quantity of sugar.

Dissolve the sugar, stirring from time to time over a low heat. Bring to a rolling boil for 2–3 minutes, test for jellying, or use the candy thermometer until it reaches 220°F.

Remove any foam from the jam, pour into hot jars, seal, cover, and label.

Cherry and Gooseberry Jam

MAKES 6–7 PT

2¼ lb sour or Morello cherries, pitted
2¼ lb gooseberries, trimmed
juice of 3 lemons
4½ lb sugar, warmed

Pit the cherries carefully over a bowl to make sure all the juice is saved. Tie the pits in a square of cheesecloth to make a bag.

Put the cherries, gooseberries, strained lemon juice, and cheesecloth bag into the preserving pan and simmer for 20–30 minutes, or until the fruit is tender. Remove the bag with the cherry pits.

Add the warmed sugar and allow to dissolve over a low heat, stirring from time to time. Bring to a boil and keep up a rapid boil for about 15 minutes. Test for jellying, or until the candy thermometer reaches 220°F.

Pour into hot jars, seal, cover, and label.

Green Gooseberry Jam

MAKES 5.6 PT

2½ lb gooseberries, washed
2½ cups water
3¼ lb sugar, warmed

Trim the gooseberries; cut in half to help the juice flow more quickly. Put in a medium-sized deep saucepan with the water, making sure there is about 3 inches depth with the fruit and water together. This will ensure that the water does not dry out (as it would in a flat preserving pan) before the skins are tender. Stew gently for about 40 minutes.

Transfer the stewed fruit to the preserving pan and add the sugar. Stir from time to time over a low heat, until all the sugar is dissolved.

If the jam looks a very pale color, you can add, very carefully, about two drops of green food coloring at this stage. Mix well and bring the pan to a rolling boil for a few minutes. Test for jellying or allow the candy thermometer to reach 220°F.

Pour into hot jars, seal, cover, and label.

Ripe Gooseberry Jam

MAKES 4½ CUPS

2¼ lb ripe gooseberries
4½ cups sugar, warmed
½ tsp Angostura bitters

Clean the ripe gooseberries, discarding any that are damaged. Chop them roughly with a sharp knife, or put into the food processor or liquidizer until roughly chopped.

Put the fruit with the sugar into a large saucepan or preserving pan, and mix well. Cook over a low heat until the sugar is completely dissolved, stirring from time to time.

Bring the pan to a full rolling boil and continue for about 4 minutes before testing for jellying, or use the candy thermometer until it reaches 225°F. Add the Angostura bitters, if using, and stir well.

Pour immediately into hot jars, seal, cover, and label.

Plum Jam

MAKES 5–6 PT

3 lb plums, washed,
halved and pitted
4 tbsp lemon juice
1¼ cups water
3 lb sugar, warmed

Crack about half the plum pits, remove the kernels, and put into a cheesecloth bag. The plums can be cut into smaller pieces, as liked.

Put the plums, lemon juice, and cheesecloth bag in the pan with the water, and bring to a boil. Lower the heat and simmer the fruit until it is tender, but not mushy.

Add the sugar and allow it to dissolve over a low heat, stirring from time to time.

Bring to a rolling boil for about 10 minutes, and test for jellying, or allow the candy thermometer to reach 220°F.

Allow to stand for 5 minutes, then pour into hot jars, seal, cover, and label.

Nutty Plum Jam

MAKES ABOUT 5 PT

4 lb plums
1¼ cups water
3 lb granulated brown sugar,
warmed
1 cup chopped walnuts
4 tbsp brandy

Cut the plums in half, remove the pits, and place them in a small pan. Pour the water over the pits and boil for 10 minutes. Strain liquid into the preserving pan. Add the plums and simmer for 10 minutes until soft, stirring frequently.

Add the warmed sugar and stir until completely dissolved. Boil rapidly for approximately 15 minutes, until jell point is reached or the candy thermometer reaches 220°F.

Remove pan from heat, and add walnuts and brandy. Leave to stand for 6 minutes and stir well.

Pour into hot jars, seal, cover, and label.

Green Plum Jam

This is an excellent way of using unripe plums.

MAKES ABOUT 4 QT

4 lb unripe plums
3¾ cups water
4½ lb sugar, warmed

Cut the plums in half and remove the pits. Crack about half the pits and remove the kernels.

Put the sugar and water into the preserving pan, and bring slowly to a boil. Lower the heat and stir until the sugar is dissolved. Boil the dissolved sugar and water for about 15 minutes, making sure it does not burn.

Add the fruit and kernels, and continue boiling until the jam is jellying or until the candy thermometer reaches 220°F.

Pour into hot jars, seal, cover, and label.

Plum and Elderberry Jam

MAKES 6–7 PT

2¼ lb elderberries, stems removed
1¼ cups water
2½ lb plums, pitted
4½ lb sugar, warmed

Put the prepared elderberries in a pan with ⅔ cup of the water. Bring the pan to a boil and simmer for about 5 minutes. Allow to cool, then transfer to a jelly bag or strain through a cheesecloth-lined sieve overnight.

Cook the plums with the remaining water until tender, then add the elderberry juice. Bring to simmering point, then add the sugar over a low heat and stir until dissolved.

Bring back to a boil, and allow to boil for 5 minutes. Test for jellying, or until the candy thermometer reaches 220°F.

Allow to stand for a few minutes, then pour into hot jars, seal, cover, and label.

Loganberry Jam

MAKES ABOUT 5 QT

6 lb loganberries, hulled and washed
6 lb sugar, warmed

Put the fruit into the preserving pan and place over a very low heat, stirring all the time until the juice starts to run out of the fruit. Cook the fruit until it is quite soft.

Add the warmed sugar and stir over a low heat, until it is completely dissolved. Raise the heat and bring the pan to a rolling boil for about 12–15 minutes. Test for jellying, or wait until the candy thermometer reads 220°F.

Pour the jam into clean hot jars, seal, cover, and label.

Quince Jam

MAKES 5 QT

4 lb quinces
5 cups water
2 lemons
6 lb sugar, warmed

Peel, core, and cut the quinces into cubes. Alternatively, they can be grated (this can be done in the food processor). Put into a saucepan with the water. Squeeze the lemons to remove the juice, and place the lemon shells and seeds from the squeezer in a cheesecloth square; tie into a bag and add to the quinces.

Bring to a boil and simmer gently for 25 minutes, until the fruit is tender. Add the sugar and dissolve over a low heat, stirring from time to time. Stir in the lemon juice and bring the pan to a rolling boil, until jell point is reached or the candy thermometer reads 220°F.

Pour into hot jars, seal, cover, and label.

Fruits of Summer Jam

MAKES ABOUT 5 CUPS

2¼ lb strawberries,
hulled and washed
8 oz red currants, trimmed
8 oz raspberries, hulled and washed
4½ cups granulated brown sugar

Put all the prepared fruit in a bowl and sprinkle with 2 tbsp sugar. Cover and leave overnight in the refrigerator.

Next day, transfer to a large saucepan with 4 tbsp water. Simmer gently until the fruit is tender.

Add the remaining sugar, and stir over a low heat until dissolved. Bring to a boil and keep on a rolling boil for 15 minutes, until jell point is reached or the candy thermometer has reached 220°F. Remove any foam with a slotted spoon.

Allow the jam to cool for 5 minutes. Pour into hot jars, seal, cover, and label.

Ginger Rhubarb Jam

MAKES 6 PT

4 lb rhubarb, washed and trimmed
1¼ cups water
4 tbsp lemon juice
2-inch piece of fresh ginger root, peeled
3 lb sugar, warmed
½ cup finely chopped crystallized ginger

Cut the rhubarb into pieces about 1-inch long, and put into the preserving pan with the water and lemon juice. Bruise the ginger by wrapping in plastic wrap, then pounding it with a weight. Add to the pan, and cook over a low heat until the rhubarb is soft. Remove the ginger.

Add the sugar and stir into the mixture over a low heat, until it is completely dissolved. Add the crystallized ginger, and bring the pan to a rolling boil for 10–15 minutes before testing for jellying. Alternatively, cook until the candy thermometer reaches 220°F.

Pour into hot jars, seal, cover, and label.

Apricot and Rhubarb Microwave Jam

MAKES 4 CUPS

1 lb dried apricots
2½ cups water
1 lb rhubarb, chopped into ½-inch lengths
4½ cups granulated or preserving sugar

Soak the apricots in the water for 24 hours, if time allows. Non-soak apricots are now available, but they should be soaked in the water for about 1 hour if possible. Otherwise, boil the measured water and pour over the apricots in a large bowl. then cook at high in the microwave for 3 minutes. Allow to stand for 5 minutes. In another dish, cook the rhubarb in a little water for 2 minutes, or until soft.

Drain the apricots, retaining the juice. Cook the apricots for a further 5 minutes. Add the rhubarb and mix well. Sprinkle on the sugar, mix well again, and add the juice, made up to 2½ cups with boiling water. Cook for about 10 minutes to bring to a boil. Stir well, and cook for another 10 minutes, until jell point is reached or the candy thermometer reaches 220°F. Allow to stand for 5 minutes.

Pour into the hot jars, seal, cover, and label.

Rhubarb and Loganberry Jam

MAKES ABOUT 7 PT

3 lb red rhubarb, cut into pieces
1¼ cups water
2¼ lb loganberries
5 lb sugar, warmed

Use only the red parts of the rhubarb, so weigh after preparing to make 3 lb. Put the rhubarb in the water and stew gently over a low heat, stirring from time to time, until completely tender and reduced to a pulp.

Pick over the loganberries and wash before putting into a preserving pan. Crush the fruit slightly to make the juice run. Simmer for a few minutes, pressing with a wooden spoon, then add the rhubarb and mix the two fruits over a low heat.

Add the sugar and mix well. Stir over a low heat from time to time, until the sugar dissolves completely. Bring to a rolling boil and test for jellying after about 5 minutes. Alternatively, use the candy thermometer until it registers 220°F.

Pour into hot jars, seal, cover, and label.

Tangy Rhubarb Orange Jam

MAKES ABOUT 4½ PT

3 lb rhubarb, cut into pieces
6 tbsp lemon juice
3 lb sugar
3 oranges
water

Wash the rhubarb, then put in a large bowl with the lemon juice and sugar. Cover with plastic wrap or a clean tea towel, and allow to stand for 24 hours. Put the whole oranges in a pan, cover with water, and simmer over a low heat until tender. Remove from the pan and cool. Cut each in half and squeeze out the juice and the seeds. Cut the peel into thin slices, and place in the preserving pan with the orange juice.

Add the rhubarb with the sugar and allow to dissolve over a low heat, stirring from time to time.

Bring to a rolling boil and continue boiling until jell point is reached, or the candy thermometer reaches 220°F.

Pour into hot jars, then seal, cover, and label.

Dried Apricot Jam

This jam is really simple to make and delicious. It can be used sieved for topping fruit tarts or any dish that requires an apricot glaze.

MAKES ABOUT 5 PT

1 lb dried apricots
7½ cups water
2 tbsp lemon juice
3 lb sugar, warmed
¼ cup blanched almonds (optional)

Place the apricots in a large bowl and cover with the measured water (make sure they are completely covered). Allow to soak for 24 hours. If using the non-soak dried variety now available, leave in the water for about 1 hour. If liked, chop into pieces.

Transfer the apricots to the preserving pan with the water and simmer for about 40 minutes, or until the apricots are tender. Add the lemon juice after about 20 minutes, or when the fruit begins to soften.

Add the sugar and stir, from time to time, over a low heat until dissolved. Add the blanched almonds, if using. Bring to a boil and continue to boil for 15 minutes. Test for jellying, or use the candy thermometer – 220°F. Pour into the hot jars, seal, cover, and label.

Apricot Jam

MAKES 5 PT

3 lb apricots, halved and pitted
1¼ cups water (add more if fruit is hard)
4 tbsp lemon juice
3 lb sugar

Take the apricot pits and crack about half of them open to reveal the kernels. Put these in boiling water and blanch for 2–3 minutes. Wrap in a cheesecloth square and tie like a bag.

Place the halved apricots in a large pan with the water, lemon juice, and kernels. Cover the pan and stew the fruit gently over a low heat until tender. Remove the bag of kernels.

Add the warmed sugar, and stir over a low heat until it is completely dissolved. Bring to a boil and keep on a rolling boil for about 15 minutes. Test for jellying or use the candy thermometer to check when it reaches 220°F. Pour into the hot jars, seal, cover, and label.

Apple and Apricot Jam

MAKES 5 PT

2¼ lb fresh apricots,
halved and pitted
2¼ lb cooking apples,
peeled and cored
2½ cups water
4½ lb sugar, warmed

Put the halved apricots into the preserving pan. Slice the apples and add to the pan with the water. Simmer for about 20 minutes, until the fruit is tender.

Add the warmed sugar and stir, from time to time, until it is completely dissolved. Bring to a boil and cook for about 15 minutes, until jell point is reached or the candy thermometer reaches 220°F.

Pour into hot jars, seal, cover, and label.

Pear and Apricot Jam

MAKES 6–7 PT

1 lb dried apricots, cut in half
3¾ cups water
3 lb pears, peeled and sliced
juice of 2 lemons
3½ lb sugar, warmed

Soak apricots overnight, or use the non-soak variety now available. If using non-soak, allow the apricots to soak in the measured water for about 1 hour. Put the drained apricots into the preserving pan with the sliced pears, lemon juice, and half the strained water. Bring to a boil, and then lower the heat and simmer for about 30 minutes, until tender.

Add the sugar and stir, from time to time, over a low heat until the sugar is completely dissolved. Bring to a rolling boil, and test for jellying after 5 minutes or when the candy thermometer reaches 220°F.

Allow to stand for 5 minutes, then pour into hot jars, seal, cover, and label.

Gingery Pumpkin and Apricot Jam

MAKES 6 PT

1 lb dried apricots, halved
2¼ lb pumpkin flesh (weight after
removing skin and seeds)
5 cups sugar
1 tbsp chopped crystallized ginger

Put the halved apricots in a bowl, just cover with water, and allow to stand for 24 hours. Place the pumpkin flesh in another bowl and sprinkle with 3 cups of the sugar. Allow the pumpkin to stand for 24 hours.

Put the apricots, with the liquid from the bowl, the pumpkin with its sugary juice, and the remaining sugar in the preserving pan with the chopped ginger. Stir over a low heat until the sugar has completely dissolved. Bring to a rolling boil until the jell point is reached, or the candy thermometer reads 220°F.

Allow to stand for 5 minutes, then pour into hot jars, seal, cover, and label.

Apple Ginger Jam

MAKES 5 PT

3 lb apples
2½ cups water
grated zest of 1 orange
grated zest of 1 lemon
2 tbsp ground ginger or finely chopped
preserved ginger
5 tbsp lemon juice
3 lb sugar, warmed

Prepare the apples by peeling, coring, and slicing. Retain all the skin and core, place in a cheesecloth square, and tie into a bag.

Place the apples, water, cheesecloth bag, zest, and the ginger in a large pan, and stew until the fruit is tender.

Remove the bag and add the lemon juice to the fruit before adding the sugar.

Dissolve the sugar over a low heat, stirring from time to time. Bring to a rolling boil and stir, from time to time, until jellying stage is reached (about 15 minutes) or until the candy thermometer reaches 220°F.

Pour into hot jars, seal, cover, and label.

Autumn Fruit Jam

Make the jam in the autumn when apples and pears are plentiful.

MAKES ABOUT 5 PT

1 lb cooking apples, peeled and cored
1 lb pears, peeled and cored
1 lb plums, halved and pitted
1½-inch piece fresh ginger root,
peeled and bruised
1¼ cups water
grated zest and juice of 1 lemon
about 3 lb sugar

Prepare the fruits (retain the plum pits) and ginger (bruise the ginger by hitting it with a rolling pin or meat pounder). Put the fruit and ginger into the preserving pan with the water and lemon juice. If liked, put the pits and the lemon zest into a cheesecloth square, tie into a bag, and add to the pan. Bring the pan to a boil, and simmer the fruit until it is tender.

Tip the stewed fruit into a large bowl or saucepan and measure back into the preserving pan. Squeeze out the cheesecloth bag, remove the bag and the ginger. For each cup of stewed fruit, allow ⅔ cup of sugar, and stir over a low heat until the sugar is dissolved.

Bring up to a rolling boil and continue to cook for about 10 minutes, until jelling point is reached or the candy thermometer reaches 220°F.

Pour into hot jars, seal, cover, and label.

Blackberry and Apple Jam

MAKES 5 QT

4 lb blackberries
1¼ cups water
4 lb cooking apples, peeled,
cored, and sliced
6 lb sugar, warmed

Place the blackberries in a large saucepan with half the water, and cook gently until soft. Put the apples with the remaining water in the preserving pan, and cook over a gentle heat until tender.

Add the cooked blackberries (they may be sieved and added as a puree if a smooth jam is preferred). Sprinkle on the warmed sugar and stir, from time to time, over a low heat until dissolved. Bring to a boil for about 15 minutes, until jelled or until the candy thermometer reaches 220°F.

Pour into the hot jars, seal, cover, and label.

Autumn Pear and Apple Jam

MAKES 6–7 PT

*2¼ lb cooking apples,
peeled and cored
2¼ lb pears, peeled and cored
1 small cinnamon stick
scant 2 cups water
4 lb sugar, warmed
finely grated zest and juice of 2 lemons*

Prepare the fruit and cut into small pieces.

Put the cinnamon stick and the water in a small pan, and allow to simmer for about 20 minutes.

Put the sugar in the preserving pan, and strain the water from the small pan onto the sugar. Mix well and stir over a low heat until dissolved. Add the zest and the strained lemon juice, then add the apples and pears. Bring the pan to a rolling boil and continue to boil for about 15 minutes, and then test for jellying. If using a candy thermometer, it should reach 220°F.

Pour into hot jars, seal, cover, and label.

Vanilla Pear Jam

An excellent way to use up excess pears if you have a pear tree. Make the jam just as the pears are beginning to ripen. If you don't have a tree, halve the ingredients for a smaller quantity.

MAKES ABOUT 5 QT

*10 lb pears
2 tsp tartaric acid
about 8 lb sugar
1 vanilla bean*

Peel and core the pears, then cut into small pieces with a sharp knife or use the thick slicing blade on the food processor. Put in the preserving pan and cover with boiling water. Simmer until tender, then strain the water off into a pan or jug.

Weigh the cooked fruit and allow 1 lb of sugar to every 1 lb fruit. Put the sugar into a preserving pan and add 1¼ cups pear water. Dissolve the sugar slowly over a low heat.

Add the cooked pears and the vanilla bean. Bring the pan to a rolling boil, and keep boiling until the jam is golden brown and thick like marmalade. Test for jellying, or use the candy thermometer until it reads 220°F.

Pour into hot jars, seal, cover, and label.

Spiced Peach Jam

MAKES 6 PT

*1 cooking apple, sliced and chopped with core
zest of 2 lemons, finely peeled
2 cloves
3½ lb ripe peaches,
pitted and sliced
2 tbsp lemon juice, optional
1¼ cups water
1 tsp allspice
3½ lb sugar, warmed*

Make a square with a tripled piece of cheesecloth, and place the apple with seeds and core on the cheesecloth with the lemon zest and the cloves; tie into a bag.

Place the peaches into the pan with the water and the cheesecloth bag. Two tbsp of lemon juice can be added at this stage, if liked.

Bring the peaches to a boil, then turn down the heat and allow the fruit to simmer until soft. Add the warmed sugar, and stir over a low heat until it is completely dissolved.

Turn up the heat until the contents of the pan are boiling rapidly. Continue to boil for about 15–20 minutes, until jell point is reached or the candy thermometer has reached 220°F.

Pour into hot jars, seal, cover, and label.

Golden Pineapple-Lemon Jam

MAKES ABOUT 6 PT

3 lemons
3 lb fresh pineapple flesh,
cut into pieces
2½ cups water
3 lb sugar, warmed

Squeeze the lemons to obtain maximum juice. Put all the seeds and flesh from the squeezer into a square of cheesecloth with the halved shells. Tie into a bag.

Put the lemon juice and the pineapple in the pan with the water and the cheesecloth bag. Bring to a boil, and simmer the covered pan until the pineapple is tender. Remove the cheesecloth bag and squeeze against the side of the pan to remove all juice.

Add the sugar and stir, from time to time, over a low heat until it is completely dissolved.

Bring the pan to a rolling boil and continue to boil, without stirring, for about 15 minutes. Test for jellying, or allow the candy thermometer to reach 220°F.

Leave the jam to stand for 5 minutes before pouring into hot jars. Seal, cover, and label.

Pear, Pineapple, and Lemon Jam with Kirsch

MAKES ABOUT 6 PT

3 lb pears, peeled
1 small pineapple, peeled and cored
juice and peel of 5 lemons
4 lb sugar, warmed
4–6 tbsp Kirsch

Cut the pears into slices and chop again. Chop the pineapple into pieces. Put all the fruit with the lemon juice in the pan. Place the shells of the lemons in a cheesecloth bag, tie, and add to the fruit. Bring to a boil, lower the heat, and simmer for about 10–15 minutes until the fruit is tender.

Add the sugar to the fruit and stir, from time to time, until it is completely dissolved. Bring the pan to a rolling boil and continue to boil until jell point is reached, or the candy thermometer has reached 220°F.

Pour into hot jars, seal, cover, and label.

Eggplant Jam with Pecans

MAKES ABOUT 6 CUPS

2¼ lb eggplants
1¼ cups water
4½ cups sugar, warmed
4 tbsp chopped pecans

Cube larger eggplants; otherwise, leave small ones whole. Put into a saucepan with the water. Bring to a boil and simmer over a low heat until the vegetables are tender, about 1 hour. Most of the water will have evaporated. Add the sugar and stir, from time to time, over a low heat until the sugar is completely dissolved. Bring to a boil and stir in the pecans. Test for jellying after about 5 minutes or when the mixture looks thick, or use the candy thermometer until it reaches 220°F.

Pour into the hot jars, seal, cover, and label.

CHAPTER TWO

Conserves
and
Preserves

~

These are slightly sweeter and less jelled than jam. They are often made with more exotic fruits, such as pineapple, banana, and melon. The main difference appears to be that the texture is rather more lumpy than jam. In days gone by, these were probably eaten with a spoon as a dessert as much as being spread on scones or bread.

Orange and Walnut Conserve

MAKES ABOUT 8 CUPS

2 lb large sweet oranges, washed
7½ cups water
4 cups sugar
½ cup seedless raisins
½ cup walnut pieces

Grate the peel of the oranges finely, avoiding the white pith. Cut the fruit up, and put in a pan with the water. Bring to a boil, then lower the heat and simmer for at least 30 minutes.

Strain the pulp through a coarse sieve and measure the amount. You will need 5 cups of orange liquid (make up the quantity with orange juice or water, if necessary).

Add the sugar, stirring from time to time until completely dissolved.

Add the grated peel of the orange and the raisins, then bring to a boil for about 20 minutes, stirring often.

Test for jellying, and then stir in the walnuts before pouring into hot jars. Seal, cover, and label.

Plum, Brandy, and Walnut Conserve

MAKES ABOUT 7 PT

4 lb plums, halved and pitted
1¼ cups water
3 lb sugar
1 cup chopped walnuts
4 tbsp brandy

Place the plum pits in a small saucepan, cover with water, and bring to a boil for 10 minutes.

Strain the liquid into the preserving pan, add the plums, and simmer until tender, about 10–15 minutes, stirring from time to time.

Add sugar and stir over a low heat until dissolved. Bring to a rolling boil and cook for about 10 minutes, until jell point is reached or the candy thermometer shows 220°F. Remove the pan from the heat, and mix in the walnuts and the brandy.

Allow to stand for 5 minutes, pour into hot jars, seal, cover, and label.

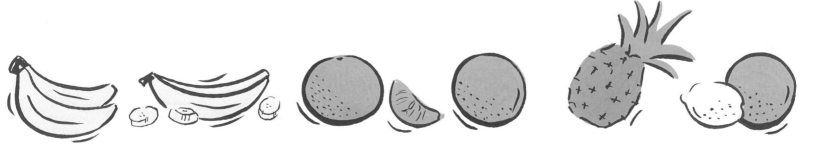

Strawberry Conserve

MAKES 5 QT

4 lb strawberries
4 lb sugar

Arrange the strawberries in a dish or bowl in layers with the sugar. Cover with plastic wrap and allow to stand for 24 hours.

Next day, transfer to a preserving pan. Bring to a boil slowly, and then boil for 5 minutes. Return to the bowl, cover, and allow to stand for another 48 hours.

Return to the preserving pan, bring to a boil, and continue cooking this way for about 15–20 minutes, until jell point is reached.

Cool slightly, stir, and then pour into hot jars. Seal, cover, and label.

Rose Petal Conserve

MAKES ABOUT 2 CUPS

2 cups preserving sugar
1 tbsp water
1 lb rose petals, preferably deep red
2 tsp orange flower water

Put the sugar in a thick-bottomed saucepan with the water. Allow the mixture to dissolve slowly over a low heat, and then simmer until it becomes a syrup.

Wash the rose petals gently and dry in paper towels. Then add them to the syrup with the orange flower water.

Simmer the mixture until it thickens slightly, but it will always be a thick syrup as opposed to a jam.

Pour into hot jars, seal, cover, and label.

Store in the refrigerator, and serve with ice cream, muffins, or scones.

Saucy Rhubarb and Carrot Conserve

MAKES 6 CUPS

1 lb tender young carrots
1 lb young rhubarb, washed
4 oz candied citrus peel
1 lemon
4½ cups sugar, warmed
1 tbsp chopped crystallized ginger

Peel the carrots and cut into pieces. Cut the rhubarb into pieces 1-inch long. Chop the citrus peel finely.

Grate the peel of the lemon, and cut away the white pith. Put the pith and seeds into a cheesecloth square, and tie into a bag.

Put the carrots, rhubarb, lemon flesh, and cheesecloth bag in just enough water to cover, and simmer until tender. Add the sugar, and stir over a low heat until completely dissolved.

Add the citrus peel, lemon peel, and chopped ginger before bringing the pan to a rolling boil. Continue until jell point is reached, or the candy thermometer reaches 220°F.

Pour into hot jars, seal, cover, and label.

Rhubarb and Orange Conserve

MAKES ABOUT 4 ½ PT

3 lb rhubarb, washed
3 lb sugar
6 tbsp lemon juice
zest and juice of 2 oranges

Cut the rhubarb into short lengths, and arrange in a bowl in layers with the sugar and lemon juice. Cover with plastic wrap or a saucepan lid, and allow to stand for 24 hours.

Next day, transfer to the preserving pan, and add the zest and juice of the oranges. Stir over a low heat until the sugar is dissolved.

Raise the heat and boil rapidly until a jam-like consistency is obtained, but the conserve will not jell like jam.

Pour into hot jars, seal, cover, and label.

Once opened, store in the refrigerator.

Rhubarb, Orange, and Brandy Preserve

MAKES ABOUT 7 CUPS

2 lb rhubarb, trimmed
4 ½ cups granulated brown sugar
2 lemons
1 orange
1 ¼ cups water
dollop of butter
3 tbsp brandy or whiskey

Cut the rhubarb into pieces 1-inch long. Arrange in layers in a bowl with the sugar. Leave to stand overnight. Add the squeezed juice of the lemons to the rhubarb.

Transfer the debris and seeds from the squeezer into a cheesecloth square laid on a plate. Finely shred the lemon peel and pith into a small pan. Peel the orange and cut the segments away from the membrane. Add the seeds to the cheesecloth, and tie into a bag Add chopped orange segments to the rhubarb.

Shred the orange peel, add to the lemon peel in the pan, and add water and cheesecloth bag. Simmer gently, covered, for about 1 hour, until tender and liquid is well reduced (more water may be needed).

Put rhubarb mixture and citrus peel into a preserving pan, and stir over a low heat, without boiling, until sugar dissolves. Bring to a full rolling boil, add the butter, and, at jell point, stir in brandy or whiskey.

Pour into hot jars, seal, cover, and label.

Honeyed Kumquat Preserve

This is a preserve which is best when eaten with a spoon and accompanied by lemon tea.

MAKES ABOUT 4–5 CUPS

1³⁄₄ lb kumquats, washed
2¹⁄₂ cups water
1¹⁄₄ cups sugar
scant ²⁄₃ cup honey

Do not peel the kumquats, but make a small incision at the tip of each.

Bring the water, sugar, and honey to a boil in a saucepan. Add the kumquats, and cook over a low heat until tender and almost transparent (about 1 hour).

Cool, then put into hot jars, seal, cover, and label.

Rich Fig Preserve

MAKES ABOUT 6 CUPS

2 lb green figs, stems removed
4¹⁄₂ cups sugar
zest and juice of 1 lemon

Put the whole figs into a large mixing bowl. Boil some water and allow to stand for a few minutes. Pour the hot water over the figs and leave to soak for about 4 minutes. Drain the figs into a colander and, when cool, transfer to a cutting board and cut up into small pieces.

Weigh the figs, and put into the preserving pan or large saucepan with the same weight of sugar. Add the zest of 1 lemon and 3 tbsp of juice. Place the pan over a low heat and allow the sugar to dissolve for about 1 hour, or until a thick, clear syrup appears. Add a small amount of water if the mixture becomes too thick.

Remove from the heat and, unlike other fruit jams and preserves, allow to become cold before putting into dry, sterilized jars.

Seal, cover, and label.

Guava and Walnut Preserve

MAKES 2–3 CUPS

1 lb guavas
2 tbsp lemon juice
1¹⁄₂ cups water
2 cups granulated brown sugar
¹⁄₄ cup roughly chopped walnuts

Peel the guavas thinly, discarding the ends. Cut into quarters, and then cut into small pieces. Put into a pan with the lemon juice and water. Cook gently for about 30 minutes, until the guavas are soft and the liquid is reduced. Rub the pan contents through a sieve to remove the seeds.

Measure the puree and make up to 2¹⁄₂ cups with water. Pour the puree into the cleaned pan over a low heat, then add the sugar. Stir over the low heat, without boiling, until the sugar is completely dissolved. Bring to a boil and stir frequently, until thick and creamy, then stir in the walnuts.

Pour into hot jars, seal, cover, and label.

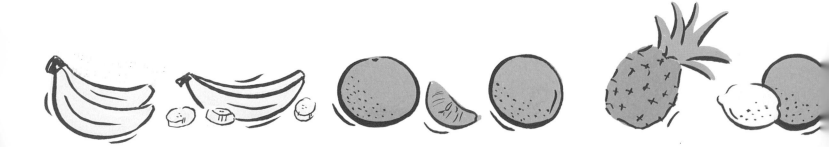

Nectarine and Passion Fruit Preserve

MAKES 4–5 CUPS

3 lb nectarines
6 tbsp lemon juice
8–10 passion fruit
1¼ cups water
4½ cups granulated brown sugar

Skin the nectarines, remove the pits, and cut the fruit into small pieces. Put into a pan with the lemon juice.

Cut the passion fruit in half, scoop out the seeds and flesh, and quarter the skins. Tie the passion fruit flesh and skins in cheesecloth, and add to the pan. Pour in the water and cook gently for about 30 minutes, until the nectarines are soft and the liquid is reduced. Remove the cheesecloth and squeeze the juice into the pan. Add the sugar and stir over a low heat, without boiling, until completely dissolved. Bring to a boil and boil briskly until jell point is reached. Leave in the pan for 10 minutes for fruit to settle.

Pour into hot jars, seal, cover, and label.

Special Pear and Apricot Preserve

MAKES 5–6 PT

8 oz dried apricots, halved
4 cups water
3 cups sugar
juice of 2 lemons
few drops of yellow food coloring
2¼ lb pears, peeled
4 tbsp Grand Marnier liqueur

Soak the apricots in the measured water for six hours, or if using non-soak, for 1 hour. Drain, retaining the water.

Dissolve the sugar in the lemon juice and the drained apricot water. Bring to a boil, and simmer until the liquid is syrupy. Add the yellow coloring to tint the syrup.

Cut the pears into thick slices, and add to the pan with the halved apricots. Bring to a boil, and then turn the heat down and simmer gently until the fruit is tender.

Bring to a boil again, and add the Grand Marnier. Boil for a few minutes, then test for jellying or when the candy thermometer has reached 220°F. Remove any foam, and allow to stand for 5 minutes.

Pour into hot jars, seal, cover, and label.

Spiced Green Tomato Preserve

MAKES ABOUT 6 QT

3 large lemons
4 cups water
2 cinnamon sticks
5½ lb green tomatoes
4½ lb granulated brown sugar, warmed

Wash and dry the lemons, cut into quarters lengthwise, and discard the seeds. Slice very thinly across, retaining as much juice as possible. Put into a pan with water, and cook gently for about 30 minutes until soft.

Strain, measure the liquid, and make up to 1¾ cups with more water. Return measured liquid to pan with cooked lemon and the cinnamon sticks.

Wash and dry the tomatoes, and cut into fairly small pieces, removing stem ends.

Add to pan, and cook gently for about 1 hour, until tomatoes are soft and the liquid has evaporated. Remove cinnamon, add sugar, and stir over a low heat until completely dissolved.

Pour into hot jars, seal, cover, and label.

Lemony Melon Preserve

MAKES ABOUT 8 CUPS

*1 large firm-fleshed melon or
3 lb melon flesh
zest and juice of 2 lemons
3 lb sugar
1 bottle commercial pectin (follow
manufacturers' directions)*

Remove the flesh from the melon, discard the seeds, and cut the flesh into cubes. Put the melon in a large pan with the zest and juice of the lemons. Bring to a boil, turn the heat low, and simmer, covered, for about 20 minutes until the melon is translucent.

Add the sugar and dissolve over a low heat, stirring from time to time. Bring to a full rolling boil for 2–3 minutes, remove from the heat, and stir in the pectin.

Allow to cool, pour into hot jars, seal, cover, and label.

Tropical Banana-Date Preserve

MAKES ABOUT 6 CUPS

*3 cups peeled, cored, and diced
cooking apples
3 tbsp lemon juice
1¾ cups water
2½ cups sliced bananas
1½ cups skinned, pitted, and sliced
fresh dates
2 cups granulated brown sugar*

Put the apples in a pan, and cook with lemon juice and water for about 5 minutes until soft.

Stir both the bananas and dates into the apple. Continue to cook for about 20 minutes, stirring often, until pulpy and the liquid is reduced to about 4½ cups.

Stir in the sugar, and dissolve over low heat, stirring all the time. Bring to a boil, stirring frequently, and boil gently until thick and the spoon leaves a space when pulled through center. This will take 45–60 minutes.

Pour into hot jars, seal, cover, and label. Eat within two months, and once open, store in the refrigerator.

Banana-Cinnamon-Rum Preserve

MAKES ABOUT 6 PT

*4½ lb bananas
(about 3 lb peeled)
zest and juice of 2 lemons
2 tbsp rum
2 tsp ground cinnamon
3 lb sugar*

Slice the peeled bananas into a bowl, and add the lemon zest, juice, and rum. Turn over with a fork to coat as much as possible. Layer the banana mixture with the sugar in a large bowl. Cover with plastic wrap, and leave to stand for 24 hours.

Next day, transfer to the preserving pan, and flavor with the cinnamon and sprinkle on the remaining sugar. Stir gently over a low heat, until the sugar is completely dissolved.

Bring to a rolling boil for about 5 minutes, stirring until thick and the mixture is a rich brown color. Remove from the heat, and allow to stand until the conserve thickens.

Pour into hot jars, seal, cover, and label.

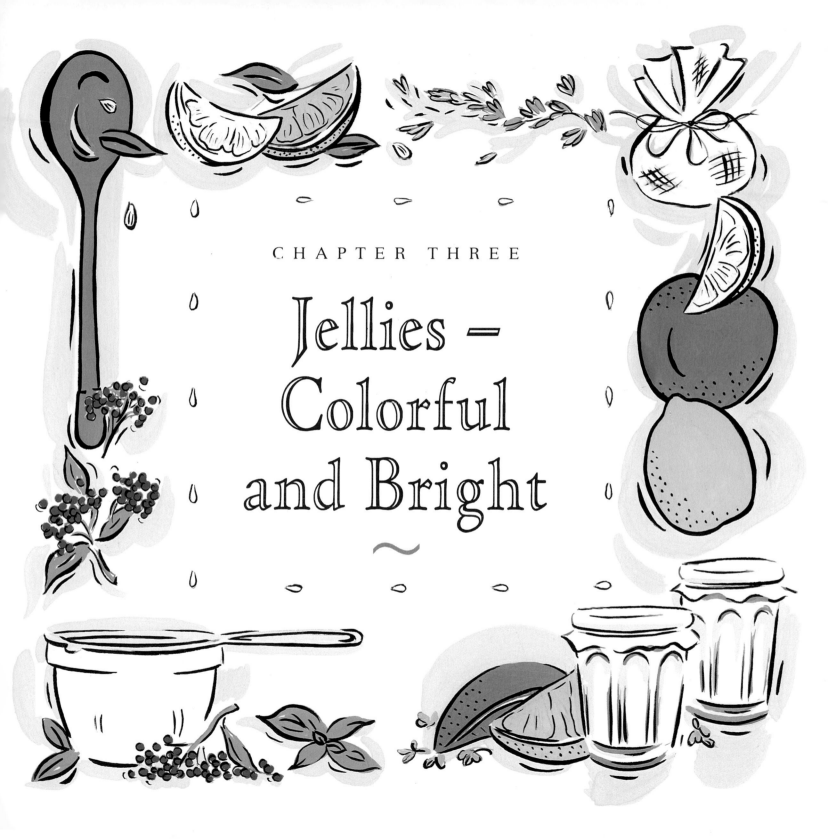

CHAPTER THREE

Jellies –
Colorful
and Bright

~

To MAKE JELLY, follow the basic rules of jam-making and testing. The main difference is the amount of sugar used for jelly, as this is calculated on the amount of fruit juice that is strained from the fruit. This is why the jelly recipes give an approximate amount of sugar as a guide.

Preparation for jelly-making is much easier than for jam because all the washed fruit is stewed with skins, pits, and cores. The fruit must be soft and mushy before straining. However, it must be remembered that the juice is strained for several hours, and should be kept in a safe place away from children or animals. It is best to shut the fruit in a room overnight to avoid spillage.

EQUIPMENT FOR JELLY-MAKING

Again, the equipment is exactly the same as for jam (*see* pages 8–9), with the exception of the jelly bag. This is a muslin bag which can be hung over a bowl to allow the long slow dripping the fruit juice requires. These bags can be hung from an upturned stool or chair, often slung through a wooden broom handle. They are available in good kitchen stores. If no jelly bag is available, then use a large sieve with several layers of cheesecloth. Tie the fruit in the cheesecloth like a bag, and rest it in the sieve.

GENERAL GUIDELINES

For fruit high in pectin, 4 cups sugar is used to each 4 cups juice. Fruits lower in pectin will use slightly less.

Do not, in any circumstances, squeeze the bag to hurry the fruit juice, or else the jelly will be cloudy.

Remove foam before canning, or the appearance of the jelly will be impaired.

Do not tilt jelly in jars before it is cool and set.

Apple and Lemon Jelly

MAKES ABOUT 8 CUPS

6 lb apples, washed
3 lemons
10 cups water
about 4 lb sugar

Remove any damaged parts of the apples and cut into pieces, including the cores and skins. With a sharp knife, peel the lemons thinly, and then squeeze out the juice.

Put the apples, lemon peel, and juice into the preserving pan with the water. Bring to a boil slowly, then reduce the heat and simmer gently until the fruit is tender.

Scald the jelly bag and add in the apple and lemon mixture. Allow to strain slowly, without squeezing the bag.

Measure the apple juice into the preserving pan again, and add 2 cups sugar for every 2½ cups of juice. Allow the sugar to dissolve over a low heat, stirring from time to time.

Bring the pan to a rolling boil, and test for jellying after 10 minutes, or when the candy thermometer reaches 220°F.

Pour into hot jars, cover, seal, and label.

Jelly Marmalade

MAKES ABOUT 5 PT

2 lb Seville oranges
2 lemons
11 cups water
about 3 lb sugar

Wash the fruit and dry with paper towels. Remove the peel thinly from the oranges and lemons with a vegetable peeler. Cut into thin strips to be used in the marmalade later, and put in a cheesecloth square, tied into a bag. Put into a pan with 2½ cups water, and cook gently for about 1½ hours, covered if possible.

Squeeze the juice from the halved lemons.

Cut the remainder of the fruit, including what remains of the lemons, into pieces, and place in a large saucepan with a lid. Add 6 cups water and cook, covered, for about 2 hours.

Scald the jelly bag with boiling water and strain the contents of both saucepans for 30 minutes, retaining the cheesecloth bag.

Return the contents of the jelly bag to the preserving pan, add the remaining 2½ cups of water, and simmer for a further 30 minutes.

Transfer the contents of the pan back to the jelly bag, and allow to drip overnight.

Measure all the strained juice back into the preserving pan, and add 2 cups sugar to every 2½ cups juice. Dissolve the sugar over a low heat, stirring from time to time.

Bring to a rolling boil for about 10 minutes, and add some of the thinly sliced shreds of peel from the cheesecloth bag. Test for jellying, or use the candy thermometer until it reaches 220°F.

Pour into hot jars, seal, cover, and label.

Seville Orange Jelly

MAKES ABOUT 5 PT

2½ lb Seville oranges
2 small lemons
9 cups water
about 3 lb sugar

Remove the peel from the oranges and lemons with a vegetable peeler. Remove the seeds (over a bowl to catch the juice), and put into a small saucepan. Cut the remaining fruit into pieces. Pour 2½ cups of the water over the seeds, and simmer for about 30 minutes. Cover, and leave until cold.

Place the lemon pieces in the preserving pan with the remaining measured water. Strain the seed water into the pan, bring the pan to a boil, and simmer for 40 minutes.

Scald the jelly bag with boiling water, and drain the fruit pulp overnight without squeezing the bag.

Measure the juice into a clean pan, and add 2 cups sugar to every 2½ cups of juice. Put the pan on a low heat, stirring from time to time, until the sugar is completely dissolved.

Bring the pan up to a rolling boil and, after 10 minutes, test for jellying, or use the candy thermometer until it reaches 220°F.

Allow to cool slightly, then pour into hot jars, seal, cover, and label.

This is best stored in small jars, to serve with poultry or duck, or to make a sauce for desserts.

Lemon Jelly

This is delicious as a sauce for sponge cakes and shortcake.

MAKES 5 PT

3 lb lemons
9 cups water
about 3 lb sugar

Remove the peel from the lemons with a vegetable peeler. Remove the seeds (over a bowl to catch the juice), and cut the remaining fruit into pieces. Put the seeds in a small saucepan, and pour 2½ cups of the water over them; simmer for about 30 minutes. Cover, and leave until cold.

Place the lemon pieces in the preserving pan with the remaining measured water. Strain the seed water into the pan, bring the pan to a boil, and simmer for 40 minutes.

Scald the jelly bag with boiling water, and drain the fruit pulp overnight without squeezing the bag.

Measure the juice into a clean pan and add 2 cups sugar to every 2½ cups of juice. Put the pan on a low heat, stirring from time to time, until the sugar is completely dissolved.

Bring the pan up to a rolling boil. After 10 minutes, test for jellying or use the candy thermometer until it reaches 220°F.

Allow to cool slightly, then pour into hot jars, seal, cover, and label.

Rosemary Jelly

MAKES ABOUT 7 PT

5 lb cooking apples, washed
2½ cups water
4–6 tbsp fresh rosemary leaves
1 cup cider vinegar
about 4 lb sugar
few drops of green food coloring
(optional)

Cut the apples in rough slices, and put into the preserving pan with the water. Bring to a boil, then reduce the heat, simmer for 5 minutes, and add half the rosemary leaves. Stir around and simmer over a low heat for about 30 minutes, until the apples are pulpy. Add the vinegar, and simmer for a further 5 minutes.

Scald the jelly bag with boiling water, and strain the apple and rosemary pulp through.

Measure the juice into a clean pan, and add 2 cups sugar to every 2½ cups of juice. Put the pan on a low heat, stirring from time to time, until the sugar is completely dissolved.

Bring the pan up to a rolling boil and, after 5 minutes, add the rest of the rosemary. Stir well and, if necessary, add a few drops of green coloring. Test for jellying, or use the candy thermometer until it reaches 220°F. Skim, if necessary.

Allow to cool slightly, then pour into hot jars, seal, cover, and label.

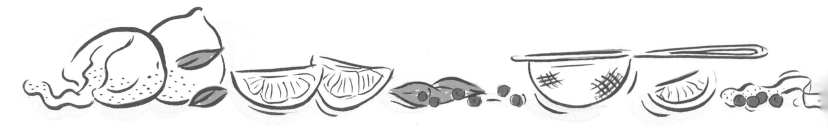

Cool Mint Apple Jelly

MAKES ABOUT 6 CUPS

4 lb cooking apples, washed
large bunch of fresh mint, washed
juice of 2 lemons
4½ cups water
about 5 cups sugar
few drops of green food coloring
(optional)

Slice the apples roughly, and put in a large saucepan with half the mint, the lemon juice, and the water. Bring to a boil and simmer for about 30 minutes, or until the apples are soft and pulpy.

Scald the jelly bag with boiling water, and strain the apple pulp through.

Measure the juice into a clean pan, and add 2 cups sugar to every 2½ cups of juice. Put the pan on a low heat, stirring from time to time.

Remove the remaining mint leaves and chop finely (this can be done in the food processor).

Bring the pan up to a rolling boil and, after 5 minutes, add the mint, stir well, and, if necessary, add a few drops of green coloring. Test for jellying, or use the candy thermometer until it reaches 220°F.

Allow to cool slightly, then pour into hot jars, seal, cover, and label.

Gooseberry and Mint Jelly

MAKES ABOUT 5 PT

4 lb gooseberries, washed
large bunch of fresh mint, washed
4 cups water
about 3 lb sugar
few drops of green food coloring
(optional)

Put the washed gooseberries in a large saucepan with half the mint, the lemon juice, and the water. Bring to a boil and simmer for about 30 minutes, or until the fruit is soft and pulpy.

Scald the jelly bag with boiling water, and strain the gooseberry pulp through the bag.

Measure the juice into a clean pan, and add 2 cups sugar to every 2½ cups of juice; put the pan on a low heat, stirring from time to time.

Remove the remaining mint leaves from the stems and chop finely (this can be done in the food processor).

Bring the pan up to a rolling boil and, after 5 minutes, add the mint, stir well, and, if necessary, add a few drops of green coloring. Test for jellying, or use the candy thermometer until it reaches 220°F.

Allow to cool slightly, then pour into hot jars, seal, cover, and label.

Gooseberry and Elderflower Jelly

MAKES ABOUT 5 PT

4 lb gooseberries, washed
2 tbsp lemon juice
4 cups water
about 3 lb sugar
4 large elderflower heads, well washed

Put the washed gooseberries in a large saucepan with the lemon juice and the water. Bring to a boil and simmer for about 30 minutes, or until the fruit is soft and pulpy.

Scald the jelly bag with boiling water, and strain the gooseberry pulp through.

Measure the juice into a clean pan, and add 2 cups sugar to every 2½ cups of juice. Put the pan on a low heat, stirring from time to time.

Place the elderflowers in a cheesecloth square, and tie into a bag; add to the pan while the sugar is dissolving. Bring the pan up to a rolling boil, stir well. Test for jellying, or use the candy thermometer until it reaches 220°F.

Allow to cool slightly, then pour into hot jars, seal, cover, and label.

Gooseberry and Crabapple Jelly

MAKES ABOUT 3 PT

1 lb gooseberries, washed
3 lb crabapples, washed and halved
grated zest of 2 lemons
1 cinnamon stick
5 cups water
3–4 lb sugar

Place the gooseberries and crabapples in a preserving pan with the water, lemon rind, and cinnamon stick, and bring slowly to a boil. Reduce the heat to low, and simmer the fruit until it is tender and pulpy. Allow to cool slightly.

Scald the jelly bag with boiling water and drain the fruit pulp overnight, without squeezing the bag.

Measure the juice into a clean pan, and add 2 cups sugar to every 2 cups of juice. Put the pan on a low heat, stirring from time to time, until the sugar is completely dissolved.

Bring the pan up to a rolling boil and after 10 minutes, test for jellying or use the candy thermometer until it reaches 220°F.

Allow to cool slightly, then pour into hot jars, seal, cover, and label.

Grape Jelly

MAKES 5 PT

6 lb green grapes
1 lemon, cut into thin slices
5 cups water
about 3 lb sugar

Place the grapes and lemon slices in a large pan with the water, and bring slowly to a boil. Reduce the temperature to low, and simmer the fruit until it is tender and pulpy. Allow to cool slightly.

Scald the jelly bag with boiling water, and drain the fruit pulp overnight without squeezing the bag.

Measure the juice into a clean pan, and add 1½ cups sugar to every 2½ cups of juice. Put the pan on a low heat, stirring from time to time, until the sugar is completely dissolved.

Bring the pan up to a rolling boil and, after 10 minutes, test for jellying or use the candy thermometer until it reaches 220°F.

Allow to cool slightly, then pour into hot jars, seal, cover, and label.

Plum Jelly

MAKES ABOUT 5 PT

6 lb plums, washed
7½ cups water
about 4 lb sugar

Put the plums, whole, into the preserving pan with the water. Put the pan over a low heat, simmering for about 45 minutes, until the plums are tender and can be mashed.

Scald the jelly bag, and drain the juice through without squeezing the bag; this is best done overnight.

Measure the juice into the preserving pan and put over a low heat. Add 2 cups of sugar to each 2½ cups juice, and allow the sugar to dissolve completely over a low heat, stirring from time to time.

Bring the pan to a rolling boil for about 10 minutes. Test for jellying, or use the candy thermometer to 220°F.

Pour into hot jars, seal, cover, and label.

Red Currant Jelly

MAKES 5 QT

8 lb red currants (or a mixture
of red and white)
5 cups water
about 6 lb sugar

Wash the red currants and put in the preserving pan with the water. Put the pan over a low heat, simmering for about 45 minutes, until the currants are tender and can be mashed.

Scald the jelly bag, and drain the juice through without squeezing the bag; this is best done overnight.

Measure the juice into the preserving pan and put over a low heat. Add 2 cups of sugar to each 2½ cups juice, and allow the sugar to dissolve completely over a low heat, stirring from time to time.

Bring the pan to a rolling boil for about 10 minutes. Test for jellying, or use the candy thermometer to 220°F.

Pour into hot jars, seal, cover, and label.

Black Currant Jelly

MAKES ABOUT 5 QT

4 lb black currants
2½ cups water
about 3 lb sugar

Wash the black currants and put in the preserving pan with the water. Put the pan over a low heat, simmering for about 45 minutes, until the currants are tender and can be mashed.

Scald the jelly bag, and drain the juice through without squeezing the bag; this is best done overnight.

Measure the juice into the preserving pan and put over a low heat. Add 2 cups of sugar to each 2½ cups juice, and allow the sugar to dissolve completely over a low heat, stirring from time to time.

Bring the pan to a rolling boil for about 10 minutes. Test for jellying, or use the candy thermometer to 220°F.

Pour into hot jars, seal, cover, and label.

Gooseberry Jelly

MAKES ABOUT 8 CUPS

4 lb gooseberries, washed
7½ cups water
about 3 lb sugar

Place the gooseberries in a preserving pan with the water and bring to a boil. Lower the heat, and simmer for about 45 minutes, or until the gooseberries are tender.

Scald the jelly bag with boiling water, and strain the jelly through without squeezing the bag. This is best done overnight.

Measure the juice into the preserving pan, and for every 2½ cups juice, add 2 cups sugar. Heat the pan over a low heat, until the sugar is completely dissolved.

Bring to a rolling boil for about 10 minutes, and then test for jellying or use the candy thermometer until it reaches 220°F.

Pour into hot jars, seal, cover, and label.

Quince Jelly

MAKES ABOUT 5 PT

8 lb quinces, washed
7½ pt water
lemon juice
about 4 lb sugar

Slice the quinces finely (this can be done in the food processor, since they are very hard). Put into the preserving pan with 10 cups of the water. Simmer for about 1 hour, until the fruit is tender.

Scald the jelly bag with boiling water, and then strain the quinces through the bag for several hours. Do not squeeze the bag.

Transfer the pulp back to the preserving pan, add the remaining water, and bring to a boil. Reduce the heat and simmer for a further 30 minutes. Strain again, mixing the two batches of juice.

Clean the preserving pan, place over a low heat, and measure the juice back into the pan. For every 2½ cups juice, add 1 tbsp lemon juice and 2 cups sugar. Stir from time to time, until the sugar is completely dissolved.

Bring the pan to a rolling boil for about 10 minutes, then test for jellying or use the candy thermometer to reach 220°F.

Pour into hot jars, seal, cover, and label.

Blackberry Jelly

MAKES ABOUT 5 QT

8 lb blackberries, washed
juice of 4 lemons
4 cups water
about 6 lb sugar

Put the blackberries, lemon juice, and water in a preserving pan, and simmer until the fruit is soft and squashy.

Scald a jelly bag, and strain the juice through over a 24-hour period. Do not squeeze the bag.

Measure the juice into a clean preserving pan, and for each 2½ cups of strained juice weigh out 2 cups sugar. Put the pan containing the juice over a high heat until it boils, then lower the heat. Add the sugar, and stir in until it is completely dissolved.

Bring the pan up to a rolling boil for about 10 minutes, then test for jellying or allow the candy thermometer to reach 220°F.

Pour into hot jars, seal, cover, and label.

Apple and Blackberry Jelly

MAKES ABOUT 6 PT

2¼ lb apples
4½ lb blackberries
5 cups water
about 6 lb sugar

Wash the fruit and remove any damaged parts from the apples. Cut the apples up into slices, and put into the preserving pan with the blackberries and the water. Bring to a boil slowly, then lower the heat. Simmer the fruit until tender.

Scald the jelly bag with boiling water, and strain the fruit through without squeezing the bag.

Measure the strained juice back into the preserving pan, and add 2 cups of sugar for every 2½ cups juice. Dissolve the sugar over a low heat, stirring from time to time.

Bring to a rolling boil for about 10 minutes, and then test for jellying or use the candy thermometer until it reaches 220°F.

Pour into hot jars, seal, cover, and label.

Versatile Apple Jelly

This is the ideal jelly to make with windfalls, cooking apples, or crabapples. Extra flavorings, such as ginger, lemon zest, or cloves, can be added.

MAKES ABOUT 5 PT

6 lb apples (weight after removing
any damaged pieces)
9 cups water
juice and zest of 2 lemons
1-inch piece ginger root
about 5 lb sugar

Put the washed and cleaned apples in a large pan with the water, lemon juice, and zest. Bruise the ginger by bashing with a meat pounder, and add to the fruit. Bring to a boil, lower the heat and stew until the fruit is tender.

Scald the jelly bag with boiling water, and strain the fruit, without squeezing the bag or the jelly will cloud.

Measure the strained jelly back into the preserving pan, and for every 2½ cups juice add 2 cups sugar.

Stir, from time to time, over a low heat until the sugar is dissolved. Raise the heat and, when the jelly has reached a rolling boil, test for jellying after 10 minutes or use the candy thermometer until it reaches 220°F.

Pour into hot jars, seal, cover, and label.

Loganberry Jelly

MAKES ABOUT 5 QT

8 lb loganberries, washed
4 cups water
about 6 lb sugar

Put the loganberries in the preserving pan with the water over a low heat to simmer for about 45 minutes, until the fruit is tender and can be mashed.

Scald the jelly bag, and drain the juice through without squeezing the bag; this is best done overnight.

Measure the juice into the preserving pan and put over a low heat. Add 2 cups of sugar to each 2½ cups measured juice, and allow the sugar to dissolve completely over a low heat, stirring from time to time.

Bring the pan to a rolling boil for about 10 minutes. Test for jellying, or use the candy thermometer to 220°F.

Pour into hot jars, seal, cover, and label.

Mulberry Jelly

Mulberries are low in pectin and, even with the apple, this jelly will set lightly.

MAKES ABOUT 6 CUPS

1 lb mulberries, washed
1 lb cooking apples, washed
6 tbsp water
about 4 cups sugar

Place the fruit in a large pan with the water, and bring slowly to a boil. Reduce the temperature to low, and simmer the fruit until it is tender and pulpy. Allow to cool slightly.

Scald the jelly bag with boiling water, and drain the fruit pulp overnight without squeezing the bag.

Measure the juice into a clean pan, and add 2 cups sugar to every 2½ cups of juice. Put the pan on a low heat, stirring from time to time, until sugar is completely dissolved.

Bring the pan up to a rolling boil and, after 10 minutes, test for jellying or use the candy thermometer until it reaches 220°F.

Allow to cool slightly, then pour into hot jars, seal, cover, and label.

Quince and Apple Jelly

The fruit from the Japanese quince tree can be substituted for the quinces in this recipe.

MAKES ABOUT 7 PT

3 lb quinces, washed
1 lb cooking apples or windfalls, washed
10 cups water
juice of 1 lemon
about 4 lb sugar

Remove any damaged parts from the apples. Cut all the fruit up into rough slices, and put into the preserving pan with the water and the lemon juice. Bring to a boil slowly, then lower the heat. Simmer the fruit until tender – test by mashing with a wooden spoon.

Scald the jelly bag with boiling water, and strain the fruit through without squeezing the bag.

Measure the strained juice back into the preserving pan, and add 2 cups of sugar to every 2½ cups juice. Dissolve the sugar over a low heat, stirring from time to time.

Bring to a rolling boil for about 10 minutes, and then test for jellying or use the candy thermometer until it reaches 220°F. Pour into hot jars, seal, cover, and label.

Spiced Grape Wine Jelly

MAKES ABOUT 5 PT

3 lb green grapes
3 lb green apples
1½ lb cooking apples, washed and sliced
1 lemon, thinly sliced
1¼ cups dry white wine
6 cardamom pods
about 3 lb sugar
4 tbsp brandy

Place all the fruit in a large pan with the water, and bring slowly to a boil. Reduce the temperature to low, add the wine and cardamom pods, then allow the fruit to simmer until it is tender and pulpy. Allow to cool slightly.

Scald the jelly bag with boiling water, and drain the fruit pulp overnight without squeezing the bag.

Measure the juice into a clean pan, and add 2 cups sugar to every 2½ cups of juice. Put the pan on a low heat, stirring from time to time, until the sugar is completely dissolved.

Bring the pan up to a rolling boil, add the brandy, and after 10 minutes, test for jellying or use the candy thermometer until it reaches 220°F.

Allow to cool slightly, then pour into hot jars, seal, cover, and label.

Elderberry and Apple Jelly

MAKES ABOUT 8 CUPS

3 lb elderberries
3 lb apples
about 3 lb sugar

Strip the elderberries from the stems, and put in a pan with just enough water to cover. Bring to a boil and simmer until tender.

Cut any damaged pieces from the apples and cut into slices (include skin and cores). Cook the apples in a separate pan by covering with water and simmering until tender and mushy.

Strain the juices separately or one after the other, as preferred. Mix the juice and allow 1½ cups sugar for each 2½ cups of juice. Measure the juice and sugar back into the preserving pan.

Dissolve the sugar over a low heat, stirring from time to time. Bring the pan up to a rolling boil, and test after 10 minutes for jellying, or use the candy thermometer until it reaches 220°F.

Pour into hot jars, seal, cover, and label.

Cranberry Jelly

MAKES ABOUT 5 CUPS

2 lb cranberries
2 large oranges
1½ cups water
5 cups sugar, warmed

Remove any stems from the cranberries and rinse in cold water.

Cut the oranges into thin slices, and place in a heavy pan with the cranberries and the water.

Bring to the boil over a low heat, and simmer until the fruit is tender, about 30 minutes. Transfer to a jelly bag and allow to drain overnight.

Pour the juice back into the pan, heat slightly, and add the warmed sugar.

Stir until the sugar is dissolved, and then bring the pan to a steady boil for about 10 minutes. Test for jellying.

Pour into hot jars, seal, cover, and label.

Rowan Apple Jelly

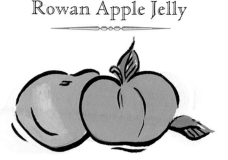

MAKES 3–4 CUPS

1 lb rowanberries
1 lb cooking apples or crabapples
5 cups water
2 cups granulated brown sugar

Strip berries free of leaves and twigs before they are weighed, then wash and dry. Scrub the apples and cut into small pieces, including skin and cores. Put all the berries and apples into a pan with the water.

Cook gently, mashing occasionally, until soft and pulpy – about 1 hour. Strain through a scalded jelly bag, overnight if possible. The juice should measure about 2½ cups. Heat it in a clean pan, add sugar, and stir over a low heat, without boiling, until completely dissolved.

Bring to a boil and boil until jellying point is reached.

Pour into hot jars, seal, cover, and label.

CHAPTER FOUR

Bittersweet Marmalades

~

THE WORD "MARMALADE" stems from the Portuguese word *marmelada*, which was a preserve made from quinces enjoyed in Europe from medieval times. In Britain, the word seems to have made an appearance around the seventeenth century. A favorite tale is told of Mary Queen of Scots being served a conserve of fruits to overcome her seasickness on the way from France, when the word was mistaken for *mal de mer*.

The preserve is now recognized as being a concoction made from citrus fruits, such as grapefruit, limes, lemons, and oranges.

Why bother to make it when you can buy so many varieties?

The really good-quality marmalades are expensive, and the homemade varieties have that extra special taste which makes the commercial products pall when tasted side by side.

WHICH FRUIT?

Bitter oranges are the most popular for marmalade in Britain, because they give a sharp tang which has been enjoyed at breakfast for many years. These oranges come mainly from Seville or Málaga in Spain, but some varieties now come from Italy and South Africa. Bitter oranges are recognizable by their dark orange color and pitted skins. The season is short and bitter oranges are available in the first few months of the year only. They will keep well in the freezer (store whole, packed in freezer bags), and you can then make your marmalade when time permits. Do buy a few extra to keep in the freezer for other times of the year because they are excellent in both sweet and savory sauces.

All citrus fruits, such as grapefruits, tangerines, and clementines, are of a good quality in the winter months of the year, so it is the best time to be making marmalade for the rest of the year. But it is always possible to have homemade marmalade at any time; just look for good-quality citrus fruit and make the Three or Four Fruits Marmalade (*see* pages 48 and 49).

EQUIPMENT

***(see also* Jam-Making, pages 8–9)**

You will need the following equipment: preserving pan (a large heavy-bottomed Dutch oven or kettle), cutting board, sharp knife, electric or hand squeezer, wooden spoon, plate, and sterilized jars, jam covers or lids, and labels.

Useful equipment, although not absolutely necessary, includes a food processor with slicing blade, a candy or jelly thermometer, and a baking sheet or plastic tray.

METHODS OF MARMALADE-MAKING

There are several methods for the keen marmalade maker to follow, and you will hear arguments for cooking the fruit whole or cutting it up, soaking or not soaking. All of these methods work well, but give slightly different results.

Marmalade does take a bit of time to prepare, and this highly satisfying task should not be undertaken when in a hurry. However, by using a microwave oven and food processor, you will be able to cut the labor down to a minimum.

Marmalade roughly follows the same rules as jam-making. However, citrus fruits contain a very high proportion of pectose (see page 9) in the pith and seeds. These need long, slow simmering in reasonable amounts of water to extract the pectin necessary for jellying the marmalade.

Citrus fruits contain a fair amount of acid, but, with the exception of lemons and limes, not enough a form a jell. Therefore, they require lemons or tartaric acid in all recipes for marmalade.

The fruit, whole or cut, can be soaked for 12–24 hours before cooking, if time is available.

Prepare the fruit by washing the skins (if they seem waxy, use a clean soft brush) and wipe with a clean cloth. It is important that the skins of citrus fruits are soft *before* the sugar is added, because the sugar will render undercooked skins tough and rubbery.

The pith of sweet oranges and grapefruit tends to cloud marmalade, and is better scraped out and cooked with the seeds in a cheesecloth bag.

Both methods of making marmalade, as well as cooking in the microwave oven, need long, slow cooking for the peels to produce pectin before the addition of sugar.

Microwave Tip

To obtain maximum juice from citrus fruits, place the fruit in a microwave oven. Allow 10 seconds per orange or fruit. This will make the fruit easier to squeeze and increase the amount of juice. Put in about 4 or 5 at a time. Cut in half, and squeeze out the juice.

Whole fruit method

1 Scrub the fruit and wipe dry with paper towels or a clean tea towel. Place in a large, heavy-bottomed preserving pan or Dutch oven. Cover with water (*see* recipes for amounts), bring to a boil, reduce heat to simmering, and allow the fruit to cook slowly for about 2 hours until the skins are soft. This can also be done by putting the oranges in a casserole dish and cooking in a low oven, after the water has been brought to a boil.

2 Drain the fruit in a colander, retaining the liquid – there should be about half the original amount left. Allow the fruit to cool because it is difficult to handle if it is too hot. Cut into quarters, and remove the seeds onto a cheesecloth square, arranged on a plate to save juice. Scrape the remaining flesh from the shells of each orange into the pan.

3 Cut the peel into thin strips with a sharp knife. Use the thinnest slicing blade on your food processor.

4 Warm the well-washed jars by placing in a low oven on several layers of newspaper. This will sterilize the jars and prevent mold forming on the marmalade during storage.

5 Place the sugar in an ovenproof bowl and put into a very low oven with the jelly jars for 20 minutes, toward the end of simmering the fruit. This helps the sugar dissolve more easily because the fruit is not cooled down by the addition of a cold mass of sugar.

6 Add the peel and the cheesecloth bag with the seeds to the pan with the orange pulp and liquid. Bring to a boil, lower the heat, and simmer for about 10 minutes. Remove the cheesecloth bag, squeezing the juice back into the pan.

7 Add the warmed sugar. Stir from time to time over a low heat, until the sugar is completely dissolved.

8 Bring the marmalade to a rolling boil and keep this brisk boil for at least 10–15 minutes, or until the mixture is jellying (*see* Jam-Making – Jellying, page 9). Alternatively, use a candy thermometer and bring the temperature to 220°F. Test for jellying as for jam (*see* page 11).

9 Allow to cool slightly in the pan before pouring into jars, to prevent the peel rising toward the surface.

10 Put the warm jars on a tray near the pan to catch the drips, and use a funnel and jug to fill with the marmalade (*see* Jam-Making, page 9). Seal immediately and label.

Cut peel method

1 Scrub the fruit and wipe dry with paper towels. Cut each in half and squeeze out the juice.

2 Arrange a square of layered cheesecloth on a plate. Transfer the seeds and pulp from the squeezer onto the cheesecloth. Tie into a bag.

3 Slice the peel with a very sharp knife into thin strips, or put through the food processor with a thin slicing blade (*see* step 3 opposite).

4 The peel, the bag of seeds, and the measured water (*see* Recipes) can be put into a large pan or bowl. Allow to steep overnight, if liked. This helps to soften the peel. However, if this is not practical, simply put all three ingredients into a preserving pan and bring to a boil. Lower the heat and simmer for 2 hours, or until the peel is softened. To test if the peel is tender, place some between two spoons and press. The peel should be fairly mushy when pressed. The liquid will be reduced by about one-third.

5 Remove the bag of seeds, squeezing well to make sure the liquid content goes into the marmalade, and continue as in the whole fruit method, above.

Sunny Plum Marmalade

MAKES ABOUT 6 PT

*3 lb plums, washed,
halved, and pitted
2 large sweet oranges
5 cups sugar
1¼ cups water*

Remove the pits from the plums, and place the pits in a cheesecloth square arranged on a plate.

Cut the oranges in half and squeeze the juice (20 seconds in the microwave for maximum juice extraction). Transfer the seeds and pulp in the squeezer into the cheesecloth. Remove as much of the pith as possible from the oranges and place in the cheesecloth. Tie into a bag. Cut the peel into thin strips.

Place the plums, orange peel, juice, and seeds into the preserving pan and pour on the water. Bring to a boil and simmer for at least 1 hour to tenderize the peel.

Add the sugar and dissolve over a low heat, stirring from time to time.

Bring to a boil when the sugar is dissolved, and boil until jell point is reached for 220°F on the candy thermometer.

Allow to cool slightly, then pour into hot jars. Seal, cover, and label.

Orange Marmalade

MAKES ABOUT 6 PT

2¼ lb Seville oranges
juice of 2 lemons
10 cups water
4½ lb sugar

Cut the oranges in quarters and remove the seeds into a bowl. Scoop out the remaining inside into another bowl. Cut the peel into very thin strips with a sharp knife. This stage can be done in a food processor with a thin slicing blade by packing the peels sideways in the tube.

Place the seeds in a sieve and strain all the juice into the measured water. Place the seeds in a cheesecloth bag. Strain the pulp in the same sieve to remove most of the juice, and place the pulp in the bag with the seeds. Tie the bag. Add the cut peel to the water, orange juice, and lemon juice. Mix well, then add the cheesecloth bag and boil until the peel is very tender. This will take at least one hour, and the liquid should be reduced by about one-third to one-half. Remove the cheesecloth bag.

Now add the warmed sugar, and stir over a low heat until the sugar is dissolved. Bring to a rolling boil, and then test after 10 minutes for a jell. Alternatively, use the candy thermometer to check when the temperature reaches 220°F.

Allow to stand for a few minutes, then pour into hot jars, seal, cover, and label.

Lime Marmalade

MAKES ABOUT 5 QT

3 lb limes
9 cups water
6 lb sugar, warmed

Cut the fruit in half (remember to put in the microwave oven, if you have one, *see* page 46) and squeeze out all the juice and seeds. Transfer the seeds from the squeezer to a cheesecloth square. Scrape the pulp out of the shells and squeezer, and chop into a large bowl. Cut the peel into thin strips and add to the pulp. Cover the contents of the bowl with the measured cold water, and soak overnight.

Put the peel and water into the preserving pan with the juice and the seeds wrapped in cheesecloth. Bring to a boil and simmer briskly for about 2 hours, until the peel is soft.

Remove the cheesecloth with the seeds, and add the sugar. Stir over a low heat until the sugar is dissolved, then bring up to a boil and allow to boil briskly, until the marmalade begins to jell when tested or has reached 220°F on the candy thermometer.

Allow to cool slightly, pour into hot jars, seal, cover, and label.

VARIATION

Lemon Marmalade

Make exactly as Lime Marmalade, substituting the same quantity of lemons for limes. Lemon and Lime Marmalade can be made using half limes and half lemons.

Three Fruits Marmalade

MAKES 5 QT

2 grapefruit (about 1½ lb)
2 sweet oranges (about 12 oz)
4 lemons
7½ pt water, warmed
6 lb sugar, warmed

Cut the fruit in half and squeeze the juice. Lay a square of cheesecloth on a plate and transfer the seeds and pulp from the squeezer. If a clear marmalade is wanted, cut or scrape some of the pith from the grapefruit and oranges, and place it in with the seeds. Tie up the four corners of the cheesecloth to make a bag.

Cut the peel into thin strips with a sharp knife, or use a thin slicing blade in a food processor.

Measure the water into the pan, and then add the peel with the juice and the cheesecloth bag to the pan, and bring to a boil. Simmer until the peel is very soft; this will take about 2 hours. The liquid will be reduced by about one-third. Remove the bag with the seeds, allow to cool, and discard the contents.

Add the warmed sugar and stir, from time to time, over a low heat, until it is completely dissolved.

Bring the marmalade to a rolling boil and continue boiling briskly until jell point is reached. This should be in about 10–15 minutes, or when the candy thermometer reaches 220°F. Test for jellying. When ready, allow to cool slightly for about 10 minutes to prevent the peel rising to the top.

Pour into hot jars, seal, cover, and label.

Bittersweet Marmalade

This is an excellent marmalade, and can be made all year-round.

MAKES ABOUT 4 QT

4 lemons
2 sweet oranges
2 grapefruit
7½ pt water
6 lb light brown sugar, warmed

Wash the fruit and dry with a clean towel or paper towels. If possible, put into the microwave oven for 10 seconds per fruit. Halve the fruit, and squeeze out all the juice.

Lay out a square of cheesecloth on a plate and transfer all the seeds onto the cheesecloth. Scrape out the white pith from the grapefruit and oranges, and put into the cheesecloth. Tie into a bag.

Cut the peel into thin strips with a sharp knife, or in the food processor using a thin slicing blade, and put into the preserving pan with the juice, the water, and the cheesecloth bag.

Bring to a boil, lower the heat, and simmer for about 2 hours. Stir from time to time. Squeeze the cheesecloth bag to remove as much liquid as possible before discarding. Add the sugar and stir over a low heat, from time to time, until dissolved.

Boil rapidly for about 15 minutes, until setting point is reached or the candy thermometer reads 220°F. Test for setting, and allow to cool slightly.

Pour into hot jars, seal, cover, and label.

Four Fruits Marmalade

MAKES ABOUT 5 QT

2 grapefruit
4 lemons
2 Seville oranges
2 tangerines
7½ pt water
6 lb preserving sugar

Remove the peel from all the fruit with a sharp knife, taking very little pith with the peel. This method is used to make a less cloudy marmalade, because the grapefruit and tangerine pith tends to cloud the marmalade. Cut the peel into thin shreds.

Lay a large square of cheesecloth on a plate. Cut the fruit in halves and squeeze out the juice. Put the pith and leftover pulp into the cheesecloth. Tie the bag. Place the peel, juice, bag, and water in a bowl, and allow to stand for 12 hours.

Transfer the contents of the bowl to the preserving pan and bring to a boil, then allow to simmer for about 2 hours.

Squeeze out the bag and discard the contents. Add the warmed sugar and stir, from time to time, until dissolved.

Bring to a rolling boil and continue to boil for 10–15 minutes, until jell point is reached or 220°F on the candy thermometer.

Allow to stand for 10 minutes, then pour into the hot jars. Seal, cover, and label.

Tomato Marmalade

MAKES 6–7 PT

4½ lb ripe tomatoes
3 lemons
4 lb preserving sugar
1¼ cups water

Place the tomatoes in a large bowl and pour boiling water over. Remove the tomatoes with a fork and pull the skins off. Slice thickly.

Slice the lemons, and remove and discard the seeds. Put the sugar in a pan with the water and bring to a boil, stirring from time to time. When dissolved, boil briskly for 6 minutes. Lower the heat, and add the tomatoes and lemons. Bring back to a boil for 30–40 minutes, until thick. Remove any foam from the surface, and the lemon peel can also be removed at the end of the cooking time with a slotted spoon.

Allow to cool slightly, then pour into hot jars, seal, cover, and label.

Grapefruit Marmalade

MAKES ABOUT 9 CUPS

2 grapefruit (about 1½ lb)
2 large lemons
7½ cups water
3 lb sugar, warmed

Squeeze the juice from the fruit (for maximum extraction, place in a microwave oven (*see* page 46). Scoop out the pulp and chop up finely. Scrape some of the pith from the lemon peels (grapefruit pith tends to make marmalade go cloudy), and put with the lemon and grapefruit seeds in a cheesecloth square, tied up like a bag. Place the fruit peel, juice, cheesecloth bag, and water into the preserving pan, and bring to a boil. Reduce the heat, and simmer until the peel is tender.

Remove the cheesecloth bag with the seeds and pith, and add the sugar. Reduce the heat and dissolve the sugar over a low heat, stirring from time to time.

When the sugar is completely dissolved, turn up the heat until the marmalade is boiling briskly. Continue to boil for 10–15 minutes, until the mixture starts to jell. Alternatively, boil until the candy thermometer reaches 220°F.

Allow to cool slightly, and then pour into hot jars. Seal, cover, and label.

Tutti-Frutti Marmalade

This mixture has a really delicate flavor, and is ideal for those who enjoy an alternative to the bitter orange flavor.

MAKES ABOUT 5 PT

1 grapefruit
1 sweet orange
1 lemon
6¼ cups water
1 large cooking apple
2 pears
3 lb sugar, warmed

If you have a microwave oven, place the grapefruit, orange, and lemon in on full power for 40 seconds. Squeeze the fruit to remove the juice, and transfer the seeds and pulp to a square of cheesecloth spread over a plate. Scrape as much of the pith from the grapefruit and orange as you can manage. Place it in the cheesecloth with the seeds, and tie into a bag.

Cut the peel into thin strips, and put into a large saucepan or preserving pan with the water and the cheesecloth bag. Bring to a boil, and then simmer until the peel is soft (about 2 hours).

Remove the cheesecloth bag, squeezing well, and add the peeled and diced apple and pear to the pan. Mix well and bring the mixture to the boil. Lower the heat and add the warmed sugar. Stir from time to time until the sugar is dissolved completely.

Bring the pan to a rolling boil and allow to cook briskly for 10–15 minutes before testing for jellying.

Allow the marmalade to stand for 5–10 minutes, then pour into hot jars. Seal, cover, and label.

Microwave Marmalade

This is an excellent way to make a small amount of marmalade. It can be made while doing other things, since there is no fear of it boiling over. This method is only slightly quicker than the conventional methods. However, the microwave oven does time the cooking for you.

MAKES 6 PT

2 lb Seville oranges
1 lemon
7½ cups water
3½ lb sugar

Place the oranges and lemon in the microwave and turn on high for 3 minutes. Cut the fruit in half and squeeze the juice. Transfer the seeds from the squeezer to a cheesecloth square placed over a plate. Scrape out any pulp left in the fruit peels with some of the pith, and put in the cheesecloth with the seeds. Tie the cheesecloth into a bag.

Cut the peel into thin strips and place in a 7½ pt bowl. Add the juice and the cheesecloth bag with the measured water. Heat in the microwave on high for about 1 hour. Stir from time to time. Test the peel to make sure that it is soft.

Stir in the sugar and put back into the microwave for 10 minutes, and then stir again. Make sure that the sugar is completely dissolved before the final boiling.

Put the bowl back into the microwave for 30 minutes on high, and then stir again. Return to the microwave for a further 15 minutes, then test for jellying. If required cook for a further 10 minutes.

Remove any foam from the surface and allow to stand for 5 minutes, then pour into warmed jars. Seal, cover, and label.

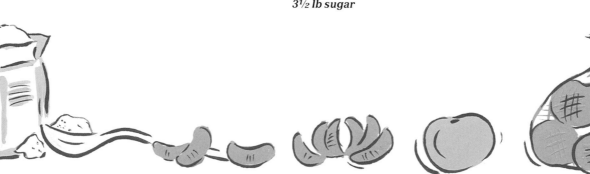

Devil's Marmalade

This is another treat for real marmalade lovers.

MAKES ABOUT 5 QT

3 lb Seville oranges
2 lemons
7½ pt water
6 lb soft dark brown sugar, warmed
2 tbsp molasses

The fruit can be treated by either method of softening, but the whole-fruit method is always successful (*see* pages 46–47). Wash the oranges and lemons and put in the preserving pan with the measured water. Bring to a boil, and simmer until the peels are soft (about 2 hours). Drain the fruit and allow to cool; retain the cooking liquid.

Cut the fruit in quarters and remove the seeds into a bowl. Scrape out the pulp into another bowl (it is best to do this because you can then catch any stray seeds). Measure 7½ cups of orange water into the pan, and add the pulp.

Scrape some of the pith into the seed bowl, and then cut the peel into thin strips and add to pulp in the pan. Add the seeds and pith wrapped in a cheesecloth bag, and bring to a boil until soft. Remove the cheesecloth bag.

Lower the heat, add the warmed sugar, and stir from time to time over a low heat until the sugar is completely dissolved. Add the molasses.

Turn up the heat, and bring the fruit and liquid to a rolling boil. Keep this brisk boil for 10–15 minutes, until jellying point is reached. Alternatively, use the candy thermometer until it reaches 220°F.

Allow the marmalade to settle off the heat for about 10 minutes, and then fill the hot jars. Seal, cover, and label.

Whiskey Marmalade

This is a slightly bitter marmalade with a whiskey flavor for the marmalade connoisseur.

MAKES ABOUT 5 PT

2¼ lb Seville oranges
1 lemon
3¾ lb preserving sugar
⅔ cup whiskey

Place the oranges and lemon in a large saucepan or preserving pan, add 9 cups of water. Bring to a boil, and simmer until the oranges are tender (about 1–2 hours).

Retain the orange water and lift the oranges and lemon into a colander. Allow to drain and cool.

Cut the oranges and lemon in half, and remove the seeds into a bowl. The flesh should be scraped out with a spoon into another bowl, and the peel placed on a cutting board. Cut the peel into thin strips. Transfer the pulp to a sieve and press any loose flesh into the juice bowl. Combine the remaining pulp and peel.

Transfer 2 cups of flesh and peel to a pan 2½ cups orange water. Add 3 cups sugar. Continue to measure out batches of solid and liquid, adding 3 cups sugar for each batch. Dissolve the sugar over a low heat, stirring from time to time.

Bring to a rolling boil and boil for about 35 minutes, until jellying or the mixture reaches 220°F on a candy thermometer. Add whiskey about 10 minutes before the end of the cooking time. Test, finally, on a chilled plate.

Allow to stand for a few minutes, then pour into hot jars, seal, cover, and label.

CHAPTER FIVE

Fruit Cheeses,
Butters,
and Curds

~

THESE ARE OLD-FASHIONED preserves made with a mixture of fruit puree and sugar. Fruit cheeses and curds have been around Britain for several hundred years and there are many old country recipes. Fruit butters are popular all over the USA, and are a particular speciality of the Pennsylvanian Dutch community.

The preserves can be served as a condiment or with cheese, and they are popular in country districts because they can be made when there is a glut of fruit. The proportion of sugar is high, but not as high as in jam-making.

FRUIT CHEESES

Fruit cheeses are usually made in molds or containers; this allows the cheese to be turned out whole and it can be served decorated with fresh fruit. Store as for jam, taking the same care with storage, and the flavor will improve with time. Serve fruit cheeses with fresh crusty bread and butter, and a favorite dairy cheese.

FRUIT BUTTERS

This is yet another way of using up excess fruit, especially apples, and the mixtures are often spiced with allspice, cloves, cinnamon, or mace.

This mixture is softer than fruit cheese, and should be kept in jars because it does not unmold like the fruit cheese. Storage periods are shorter, unless well-sealed with mason jars and processed. Keep in the refrigerator once opened, and eat within one week.

CURDS AND MINCEMEAT

These are not strictly fruit preserves, since they contain other ingredients. Fruit curds do not keep as well as jam. They should be carefully stored because they contain eggs and butter.

Once the curd is open, it should be eaten quickly or stored in the refrigerator. Curds will keep for about a month in a cool place, or for three months in the refrigerator, unopened.

Plum Cheese

MAKES ABOUT 6 CUPS

3 lb plums
²⁄₃ cup water
1 tsp allspice
sugar

Place the plums and the water in a large saucepan with a lid. Simmer the fruit for about 40 minutes, or until tender. Rub the fruit through a sieve to make a puree, and measure it back into the pan or use a preserving pan.

For every 2½ cups of puree, add 2 cups sugar. Return to a low heat and add the allspice. Mix well. Simmer, stirring all the time, until the mixture is really thick. Draw a spoon across the pan and it should leave a line.

The molds or jars should be sterilized and warm. They can be brushed with glycerin to help the fruit cheese to unmold. Seal, cover, and label.

VARIATION

Black Currant Cheese
Quince Cheese
Gooseberry Cheese
Crabapple Cheese

These are all popular country favorites which can be made using the same recipe as Plum Cheese. Other fruits can also be used.

Creamy Lemon Curd

This makes the ideal quantity for the inside of a layered cake with a little left over for a topping on scones.

MAKES 1 CUP

1 egg
juice of 1 lemon
½ cup granulated sugar
¼ cup butter

Beat egg with lemon juice and strain into a small saucepan. Add sugar and butter to the pan, and place over a low heat until butter is melted and sugar dissolved. Raise heat to low/medium, and stir constantly until mixture just starts to bubble.

Remove from the heat immediately. Pour into hot jars, seal, cover, and label.

Classic Lemon Curd

Because curd does not keep as well as jam, it is often best to store it in small jars. It can also be frozen in freezer containers for up to six months.

MAKES ABOUT 4 CUPS

grated zest and strained juice of 4 lemons
4 eggs, well beaten
½ cup softened, unsalted butter
2 cups granulated brown sugar

Put all the ingredients into a bowl standing in a pan of simmering water, or in a double boiler. Stir steadily until the sugar melts, then cook over a very low heat, stirring frequently, until the mixture thickens; do not allow to curdle.

Pour the curd into hot jars, seal, cover, and label.

Cider Apple Butter

MAKES ABOUT 6 PT

6 lb crabapples, washed
5 cups water
5 cups cider
sugar
1 tsp ground cloves
1 tsp cinnamon
½ tsp allspice
grated zest of 1 lemon

Cut any damaged parts of the fruit away and cut roughly into slices. Put the apples into the preserving pan with the water and cider. Bring the pan to a boil, and simmer until the fruit is soft and pulpy. Allow to cool slightly, and then rub through a sieve.

Measure the apple pulp back into the preserving pan, and allow 1½ cups sugar for each 2½ cups. Simmer for 10 minutes, then add the spices and grated zest, and continue cooking until thick and no liquid remains.

Pour into warm jars, seal, cover, and label.

Gooseberry Curd

MAKES 6 CUPS

3 lb gooseberries, washed
⅓ cup water
6 tbsp butter
4 eggs, beaten
2½ cups sugar

Put the gooseberries into a large saucepan with the water, and simmer until the fruit is soft and pulpy (about 25–30 minutes). Rub the gooseberries through a coarse sieve. Discard the skins.

Using a double boiler or a large heatproof bowl over a saucepan of hot water, put in the butter and allow to melt. Stir in the beaten eggs, sugar, and gooseberry puree. Whisk or stir the mixture constantly until it becomes thick.

Pour into hot jars, seal, cover, and label.

Orange Curd

MAKES ABOUT 6 CUPS

5 medium to large oranges
1 tbsp lemon juice
2 tsp orange flower water
1½ cups diced butter
4 cups superfine sugar
8 eggs, beaten

Peel the oranges, and then squeeze the juice. (If possible, microwave for 40 seconds before squeezing for maximum extraction.)

Put the juice, peel, lemon juice, orange flower water, butter, and sugar into a double boiler, or large bowl over a large saucepan half filled with boiling water, on a medium heat.

Use a whisk or electric beater and beat in the eggs a little at a time until the curd has thickened; this may take about 30 minutes.

Strain through a coarse sieve to remove the orange peel. Return to the pan, scraping as much as possible back with a plastic spatula.

Reheat for 5 minutes, then pour into hot jars, seal, cover, and label.

Cranberry Cheese

Make this fruit cheese with the extra cranberries usually around at Christmas or Thanksgiving. Serve with turkey or goose.

MAKES ABOUT 6 CUPS

3 lb cranberries
4½ cups water
3 lb sugar
zest and juice of 1 orange
2 tsp lemon juice
1 tsp cinnamon
¼ tsp mace

Rinse the cranberries, if necessary, and put into a pan covered with the water. Simmer, covered, for about 30 minutes, until the fruit is very soft. Mash the fruit with a wooden spoon or a potato masher, from time to time, to hasten the cooking and release the juice.

Put the mixture through a food processor or liquidizer. Sieve the puree into a clean pan. If there is too much liquid, boil for a few minutes to reduce.

Add the sugar, and simmer over a low heat, stirring constantly until the sugar has dissolved. Stir in the orange zest, fruit juices, and spices. Bring to a boil and cook until thick.

Put into warm molds or jars, seal, cover, and label.

Blueberry Curd

MAKES 4–5 CUPS

1 lb blueberries, washed
¾ cup butter
2 cups granulated sugar
4 medium to large eggs
few drops of red food coloring

Put the blueberries into a covered pan with 2 tbsp water, and simmer until the fruit is tender. Push through a sieve, and then pour the fruit juice into a double boiler or thick-bottomed saucepan with the butter and sugar. Stir with a wooden spoon or whisk until the sugar is dissolved.

Beat the eggs together in a bowl, and strain through a fine sieve into the blueberry mixture. Continue to stir or whisk until the contents are thick and coat the back of a wooden spoon.

Pour into hot jars, seal, cover, and label. The shelf life is the same as for Lemon Curd.

VARIATION

Blackberry Curd/ Black Currant Curd

Blackberries or black currants can also be used to make a flavored curd using the same quantities as blueberries in the above recipe.

Mixed Fruit Cheese

MAKES 6 PT

3 lb plums, washed
1½–2½ cups water
2 oranges, washed
2 cups seedless raisins
3 lb sugar

Cut the plums in half, and put into a large saucepan with the water. Slice the oranges very thinly and add to the plums. Cover, and simmer until the fruit is really soft and mushy.

Rub through a sieve and return to the rinsed pan with the sugar and raisins. Simmer until the mixture is really thick, stirring all the time.

Transfer to warmed molds or jars, seal, cover, and label.

Grapefruit Curd

MAKES 4½ CUPS

2 pink grapefruit, washed, and peel finely grated
¾ cup butter
2 cups granulated sugar
4 medium to large eggs
few drops of red food coloring (optional)

Squeeze the grapefruit, and place zest and juice into a double boiler or thick-bottomed saucepan with the butter and sugar. Stir with a wooden spoon or whisk until the sugar is dissolved.

Beat the eggs together in a bowl, and strain through a fine sieve into the grapefruit mixture. Continue to stir or whisk until the contents are thick and coat the back of a wooden spoon. Add a few drops of coloring, if liked, and stir well.

Pour into hot jars, seal, cover, and label. The shelf life is the same as for Lemon Curd.

Lemon Zucchini Curd

MAKES ABOUT 6 CUPS

2½ lb zucchini, peeled
4 cups sugar
finely grated zest of 2 lemons
½ cup butter

Cut the zucchini in quarters and remove the seeds. Weigh about 2 lb of the zucchini and boil in a saucepan with 4½ cups water and 1 tsp salt.

Strain the zucchini through a sieve, and allow to drain thoroughly. Mash the zucchini into a large saucepan. When it is pureed, add the sugar, the grated lemon zest, and the butter. Stir over a gentle heat until the butter is dissolved, then boil the marrow mixture until you have a smooth paste.

Put into small hot jars, seal, cover, and label. This curd can also be frozen in small plastic containers.

Ruby Curd

MAKES 4½ CUPS

4 blood oranges, washed and peel finely grated
¾ cup butter
2 cups granulated sugar
4 medium to large eggs
few drops of red food coloring (optional)

Squeeze the orange, and place zest and juice into a double boiler or thick-bottomed saucepan with the butter and sugar. Stir with a wooden spoon or whisk until the sugar is dissolved.

Beat the eggs together in a bowl, and strain through a fine sieve into the orange mixture. Continue to stir or whisk until the contents are thick and coat the back of a wooden spoon. Add a few drops of coloring, if liked, and stir well.

Pour into hot jars, seal, cover, and label. The shelf life is the same as for Classic Lemon Curd.

CHAPTER SIX

Chutneys

~

THIS CONDIMENT IS now popular all over the world, but originated in India with the word "chutney" coming from the Hindi word *chatni*. These savory mixtures of fruits and vegetables are preserved in vinegar, spice, and salt.

Chutneys are easy to make at any time of the year because they can be made with dried fruits, as well as fresh. There is enormous scope for imagination and individual tastes in this type of preserving because different ingredients can be used to create different flavors. Chutneys can be mild or fiery hot, depending on taste.

Dishes of chutney add piquancy to cold plates of meat or fish with salad, and they improve cheese and bread lunches and sandwiches. Curries and oriental dishes are often served accompanied by spicy chutneys.

Fruits such as apples, gooseberries, plums, peaches, apricots, and green and red tomatoes are good basic ingredients for chutney, mixed with onions, garlic, dates, raisins, chilies, spices, and sugar. The whole mixture of chosen ingredients is then preserved in vinegar. Unlike other methods of preservation, the fruit does not need to be in perfect condition, providing all damaged pieces are removed.

The onion is the toughest of the ingredients, and it is advisable to cook the prepared onion in a little water before adding the remaining ingredients. Brown sugar is often used for a dark rich color when cooking chutney. Use ground spices; otherwise, whole spices should be wrapped in cheesecloth before adding.

A good chutney should have a reasonably smooth texture with a mellow flavor. The basic ingredients can be cut up or minced fairly small (apples, plums, etc., can be chopped in the food processor for a few seconds), and ingredients such as raisins and dates will give character to the texture.

Long, slow cooking is essential for a good mellow flavor, and the chutney should be allowed to mature in the jar for at least three months.

EQUIPMENT

You will need a large pan for chutney—a preserving pan is ideal. Do not use brass, copper, or iron pans because they will react with the vinegar. Similarly, use only nylon or stainless steel sieves.

Keep one long-handled wooden spoon for chutney, because the wood will absorb some flavour and it should not be used for other cooking.

Any heatproof jars are suitable for chutney, but the best are special canning jars, such as mason jars. Wash thoroughly and dry in the oven, as for jelly jars (*see* page 11). Pour the chutney into the jars with a jug or ladle while it is hot. Seal with the sterilized metal lid, and then the screwband. If liked, process in a water-bath or steam-pressure canner (*see* page 9).

Paper covers for jars are not suitable because the vinegar will evaporate and the top of the chutney will be dried and spoiled. Use waxed paper or two layers of parchment paper to cover the chutney when it is hot. Then secure clip-on lids, or tie a piece of parchment or waxed paper around the top.

To use this method, first cover the hot chutney completely with sheets of waxed paper. Allow to cool, and then seal with plastic wrap and rubber bands. To make discs for the tops, fold a sheet of paper several times into a square and draw a circle from the top of a jar. Cut around.

Tomato Chutney with Cinnamon and Cayenne

MAKES ABOUT 4 QT

6 lb ripe tomatoes, skinned
2½ cups thinly sliced onions
4 tsp whole allspice
1 cinnamon stick
1 tsp cayenne pepper
1 tbsp salt
1¼ cups cider vinegar
2 cups light brown sugar

Cut the tomatoes in quarters and place in a large pan, together with the onions. Put the allspice and cinnamon in a square of cheesecloth, and tie into a bag. Add the cheesecloth bag, cayenne pepper, and salt to the tomato mixture. Cook gently, stirring occasionally, until the mixture is pulpy.

Add vinegar and sugar, and simmer until the mixture thickens (this may take up to an hour, but do bear in mind that tomato chutney should not be as thick as other varieties of chutney). Remove the cheesecloth bag.

Pour into hot, dry jars. Seal the jars securely, cover, and label.

Green Tomato Chutney

MAKES 5–6 PT

3 lb tomatoes, green or under-ripe
6 large onions, very thinly sliced
3 large cooking apples
2½ cups cider vinegar
1 cup raisins
2⅔ cups brown sugar
1 tsp ground ginger
1½ tsp salt
1 tsp freshly ground black pepper
4 tbsp pickling spice

Slice the tomatoes. Put the tomatoes and onions into a large bowl and sprinkle with salt. Leave overnight.

Next day, drain away juice which will have collected. Peel, core, and chop the apples. Put with the other ingredients into a large saucepan or preserving pan.

Stir over a moderate heat until the sugar dissolves, then simmer contents of pan gently for about 2 hours, or until the chutney is thick, rich, and dark brown in color.

Pour into hot jars, cover each with a disc of waxed paper and vinegar-proof tops. Alternatively, seal with metal lids and screw bands. Label with the date and allow to mature for at least three months.

Cucumber Relish with Cumin

MAKES ABOUT 8 CUPS

2 lb cucumber, unpeeled
2 Spanish onions
1 red bell pepper, deseeded
3 tbsp salt
scant 2 cups cider vinegar
2 cups light brown sugar
½ tsp turmeric
2 tsp brown mustard seeds
1½ tsp ground cumin

Thinly slice the cucumber, onions, and bell pepper (this can be done in a food processor). Layer the vegetables in a bowl and add the salt. Cover and leave for 3 hours. Transfer to a colander and rinse well.

Put in a large pan, add the cider vinegar, and bring to a boil. Simmer, uncovered, for 20 minutes, until the vegetables are tender. Stir in the sugar until dissolved. Add the turmeric, mustard seeds, and cumin, and then stir. Bring to a boil.

Remove from the heat and allow to cool. Ladle into hot jars, seal with waxed discs, and cover with plastic wrap when cold. Label.

Peppery Pumpkin Chutney

MAKES ABOUT 8 CUPS

4 lb piece of pumpkin
1½ cups skinned and chopped tomatoes
1 cup chopped onions
2 cloves garlic, crushed
4 cups light brown sugar
2 tbsp salt
1 tsp ground ginger
1 tsp black pepper
1 tsp allspice
2½ cups vinegar (white wine, cider, or rice vinegar) or distilled water

Cut the skin off the pumpkin, and remove the seeds and threads. Slice the flesh into flat pieces, about ½-inch square and ¼-inch thick. Put them into a large pan, preferably enamel or stainless steel, or a preserving pan. Add the tomatoes, onions, and garlic to the pan with the sugar, salt, spices, and vinegar or water. Allow the sugar to dissolve over a low heat, stirring all the time.

Bring the mixture to a boil, then let it simmer, uncovered, for about 1½ hours, or until it is thick and glossy-looking, like purchased chutney. It will still be runny, but will not look watery. Stir the mixture frequently toward the end of the cooking time to prevent sticking.

Pour into hot jars, and cover immediately with airtight and vinegar-proof tops. Label.

Spicy Indian Chutney

MAKES ABOUT 9 CUPS

1½ lb (prepared weight) cooking apples, peeled, cored and sliced
2 cups finely chopped onions
4 cups dark brown sugar
6¼ cups cider vinegar
2 cups chopped seedless raisins
4 cloves garlic, crushed
1 tsp salt
2 tbsp ground ginger
3 tbsp powdered mustard
2 tbsp paprika
1 tbsp coriander

Place all the ingredients in a preserving pan. Bring to a boil, then reduce the heat and simmer gently for about 3 hours, uncovered, stirring occasionally, until no excess liquid remains and the chutney is thick and pulpy.

Spoon into prepared jars, and cover immediately with airtight and vinegar-proof tops. Label.

Zucchini and Apple Chutney

MAKES ABOUT 6 PT

4 lb zucchini, peeled and chopped
5 tbsp salt
2 lb cooking apples, peeled, cored, and finely chopped
2 cups chopped shallots or onions
2⅔ cups light brown sugar
5 cups distilled white vinegar
1 tsp ground ginger
2 tbsp pickling spice

Layer the zucchini pieces into a large bowl with the salt, and leave covered for 12 hours or overnight.

Rinse the zucchini pieces, drain off the water, and put the zucchini into a preserving pan. Add the apples, shallots, sugar, vinegar, ginger, and spice. Bring to a boil, then reduce the heat and simmer gently, uncovered, for about 2 hours, stirring from time to time, until the chutney becomes thick with no excess liquid.

Pour into prepared hot jars while warm, and cover immediately with airtight and vinegar-proof tops. Label.

Tamarind Chutney

MAKES 1 CUP

2 oz dried tamarind
1¼ cups boiling water
2 tsp grated fresh ginger root
1 tbsp fresh lemon juice
1 tsp dark brown sugar
1 tsp salt
1–2 tbsp finely chopped fresh cilantro

Place the tamarind in a small bowl and pour the boiling water over it. Leave to soak for about an hour, stirring and mashing occasionally. Rub through a fine sieve, pressing down hard to extract all the pulp.

Add the ginger, lemon juice, sugar, and salt. Stir together well. Cover and store in the refrigerator, it will keep for at least a week.

Sprinkle with chopped cilantro just prior to serving.

Spiced Peach and Orange Chutney

MAKES ABOUT 7 CUPS

2¼ lb peaches, peeled,
quartered and pitted
2 onions, peeled and thinly sliced
3 large cloves garlic, crushed
grated zest and juice of 2 oranges
1 cup golden raisins
½ cup chopped preserved ginger
1 cup slivered almonds
1 tsp allspice
1 tsp cinnamon
2 tsp salt
2½ cups white wine vinegar
1⅓ cups molasses sugar

Place the peaches in a large saucepan. Add all the ingredients and stir over a low heat until the sugar is dissolved. Bring to a boil, stirring all the time. Lower the heat and simmer gently for about 1½ hours, or until the chutney is thick, stirring from time to time to avoid sticking.

Ladle into hot jars, seal with airtight, vinegar-proof covers, and label.

Red Tomato and Raisin Chutney

MAKES ABOUT 8 CUPS

6 lb red tomatoes, skinned and sliced
2½ cups minced onion
1 clove garlic, crushed
2 cups light brown sugar
2 tsp paprika
1 tsp mixed spice
pinch of cayenne pepper
1 tbsp salt
1¼ cups distilled white vinegar
1 cup seedless raisins

Place the tomatoes, onion, and garlic in a saucepan and cook gently, uncovered, until a thick puree is obtained. Add sugar, paprika, mixed spice, cayenne pepper, salt, vinegar, and raisins.

Heat gently, stirring continuously, until the sugar has dissolved. Increase the heat slightly and simmer, uncovered, stirring from time to time until the liquid is reduced – about 1 hour.

Pour into hot jars, seal with vinegar-proof tops, and label.

Apple and Mint Chutney

MAKES ABOUT 8 CUPS

4 lb cooking apples, peeled,
cored and chopped
2 onions, chopped
2 cups sugar
5 cups cider vinegar
2 cups seedless raisins
2-inch pieces ginger root, bruised
3 whole allspice
1 tsp salt
1/4 tsp cayenne pepper
6 tbsp chopped, fresh mint leaves

Place apples, onions, sugar, vinegar, and raisins in a large saucepan. Tie ginger root and allspice in a cheesecloth bag, and add to saucepan with the salt and cayenne pepper.

Heat gently, stirring continuously until sugar has dissolved. Increase the heat and simmer gently, uncovered, stirring from time to time to avoid sticking, until the mixture is thick and well reduced – about 45 minutes.

Discard the cheesecloth bag, and stir in the chopped mint; mix well.

Pour into hot jars and seal with vinegar-proof lids. Label.

Elderberry and Apple Chutney

MAKES ABOUT 6 CUPS

3 lb cooking apples, peeled,
cored and sliced
lb elderberries, stems removed
2 cups finely chopped onions
4 cups light brown sugar
4 cups cider vinegar
1/2 tsp salt
1 tbsp mustard seeds
12 whole allspice
3 small pieces ginger root, bruised
1 tsp black peppercorns

Place apples, elderberries, onion, sugar, vinegar, and salt in a large saucepan. Tie the mustard seeds, whole allspice, ginger, and peppercorns together in a cheesecloth bag. Add these to the saucepan and bring slowly to a boil, stirring continuously until the sugar has dissolved.

Simmer uncovered, stirring from time to time, until ingredients are soft and the contents of the pan are well reduced – about 1½ hours. Remove the cheesecloth bag, and press the bag through a coarse sieve.

Pour into hot jars and seal with vinegar-proof lids. Label.

Red Plum Chutney

MAKES ABOUT 6 CUPS

2 lb red plums, halved and pitted
1 lb cooking apples, peeled,
cored and chopped
2 cups chopped onions
12 peppercorns
1 cup seedless raisins
1 1/3 cup light brown sugar
2 tsp ground ginger
1 tsp ground mixed spice
2 tsp salt
1/2 tsp cayenne pepper
2 1/2 cups cider vinegar

Place the plums, apples, and onions in a large saucepan. Tie the peppercorns in a cheesecloth bag. Add to the saucepan with the remaining ingredients.

Bring slowly to a boil, stirring continuously until the sugar has dissolved. Increase the heat and simmer, uncovered, until the chutney is thick and mushy – about 1¼ hours. Remove the cheesecloth bag.

Fill the jars and seal with vinegar-proof tops. Label.

Crazy Orange and Rhubarb Chutney

MAKES ABOUT 8 CUPS

2 oranges, scrubbed
2½ lb prepared rhubarb
2 onions, chopped
5⅓ cups light brown sugar
2 cups seedless raisins
4 cups cider vinegar
1 tbsp mustard seeds
12 peppercorns
1 tsp ground allspice

Grate the peel from the oranges on a fine grater. Squeeze the oranges to extract the juice, and scoop the pulp into a bowl. Cut the rhubarb into 1-inch pieces and add to the orange with the onion, sugar, raisins, and vinegar. Put into a large saucepan with the juice.

Tie the mustard seeds and peppercorns in a cheesecloth bag. Put in the pan with the allspice and bring slowly to a boil, stirring continuously until the sugar has dissolved.

Simmer gently, uncovered, until thick and pulpy – about 1¾ hours.

Remove the cheesecloth bag, pour into warm jars, and seal with vinegar-proof tops. Label.

Sweet Pickled Orange and Lemon Rings

MAKES ABOUT 6 CUPS

3 thin-skinned oranges, scrubbed
3 thin-skinned lemons, scrubbed
4 cups distilled white vinegar
3 cups granulated brown sugar
4 tsp ground cloves
3-inch cinnamon stick
6 whole cloves

Slice the oranges and lemons ¼-inch thick. Put into a large saucepan with just enough water to cover, and simmer gently until the peel is really soft – about 45 minutes.

Remove the fruit with a slotted spoon. Add vinegar, sugar, ground cloves, and cinnamon to the juice in the pan. Bring to a boil and simmer gently for 10 minutes.

Return fruit to pan and cook gently until peel is transparent. With the slotted spoon, lift the fruit out of the syrup and pack into preheated jars. Continue boiling the syrup, uncovered, until it begins to thicken – about 15 minutes.

Leave to cool, strain, and pour over fruit. Add a few whole cloves to each jar. Cover and seal with vinegar-proof tops. Label.

Mango and Tomato Chutney

MAKES ABOUT 7 PT

3 lb unripe mangoes
2 cups finely chopped onions
1¼ cups seedless raisins
3 cloves garlic, crushed
4 yellow bell peppers, seeded and chopped
2 tbsp finely chopped, ginger root
1 tsp ground allspice
1½ lb tomatoes, peeled and chopped
1 tbsp salt
3 cups cider vinegar
4⅔ cups light brown sugar

Peel the mangoes and cut the flesh from the pits. Chop, and place in a preserving pan with the onion, raisins, garlic, bell peppers, ginger, allspice, tomatoes, salt, and vinegar. Bring to a boil, cover, and simmer for 30 minutes. Stir in the sugar and simmer, uncovered, for about 1 hour until thick. Stir from time to time.

Pour into clean, hot jars and seal with vinegar-proof tops. Cover and label.

Spicy Mango Chutney

MAKES ABOUT 4 CUPS

2¼ lb mangoes (2 large), peeled,
halved, and pitted
3 tbsp salt
6¼ cups water
1½ cups granulated sugar
2½ cups spiced vinegar
2-inch piece ginger root, peeled and
finely chopped
4 cloves garlic, finely chopped
1 tsp chili powder
1 fresh green chili, deseeded and chopped
¼ cup seedless raisins
¼ cup chopped dried dates
¼ cup dried bananas (optional)
juice of 1 lemon
1 cinnamon stick

Cut the mangoes into small pieces and
place in a large bowl with the pits.
Sprinkle with salt and cover with water.
Allow to stand, covered with a plate or
plastic wrap, for 24 hours.

Drain the mangoes in a plastic
colander or sieve, and remove the pits.

Pour the sugar and vinegar into a
preserving pan or a heavy-bottomed
saucepan. Allow the sugar to dissolve
over a low heat, stirring from time to
time, then bring to a boil.

Add all the other ingredients and mix
well. Bring back to a boil and simmer,
stirring frequently, until the chutney is
thick, about 30 minutes. Remove the
cinnamon.

Pour into hot jars, cover, and label.
Allow to mature for at least a month.

Apple, Apricot, or Pumpkin Chutney

MAKES 9 CUPS

2¼ lb apples or pumpkin, peeled,
cored or seeded, and chopped, or
1 lb dried apricots
2 cups chopped onions
1 cup seedless raisins
2½ cups white wine vinegar
2⅔ cups dark brown sugar
½ cup chopped preserved ginger
2 tsp mustard seeds
1 tsp cayenne pepper (optional)
salt
1 tsp turmeric
grated zest and juice of 1 orange
scant cup shelled walnuts

Put all the ingredients, except the
walnuts, into a pan and cook gently,
stirring over a low heat until the sugar is
dissolved. Bring to a boil, then lower the
heat and cook until a mushy consistency
(about 1½ hours).

Stir the walnuts into the mixture. Pack
into hot jars and seal. Label. Store for at
least a month before using.

Chunky Vegetable Relish

MAKES ABOUT 6 CUPS

8 oz carrots, peeled
8 oz rutabaga, peeled
1 lb cooking apples, peeled and cored
1 large onion
1 cup small cauliflower florets
½ cup golden raisins
1¼ cups brown sugar
3 tbsp tomato paste
2 tbsp lemon juice
1 clove garlic, crushed
2½ cups cider vinegar
salt and freshly ground black pepper
½ tsp ground mixed spice

Dice the carrots, rutabaga, and apple;
chop the onion. Blanch the carrots in
boiling, salted water for 4 minutes.
Drain well.

Place the carrots with all other
ingredients in a large saucepan. Bring
slowly to a boil, stirring continuously
until the sugar has dissolved. Increase
heat and simmer, uncovered, until
vegetables are just tender and contents
of pan are well reduced – about 1¼
hours.

Pour into hot jars and seal with
vinegar-proof tops. Label.

CHAPTER SEVEN

Flavored Vinegars and Oils

~

MANY VARIETIES OF herb-flavored and spiced oils and vinegars are available in supermarkets. These will enhance salad dressings, homemade chutneys, and relishes. However, if you have herbs in the garden or on the patio, you will find it easy to make your own inexpensively. Flavored oils and vinegars make excellent and welcome gifts, so make some extra to give to friends. Save any interesting bottles to store them.

VINEGAR

For more subtle flavors, use wine or cider vinegar to make dressings, although strong distilled white vinegar may be used for pickling. Try to buy large containers of vinegar or oil to make flavored products, because small bottles from the supermarket are less cost-effective.

Vinegar-proof seals are essential for bottles and jars. Use new corks or caps, or waxed paper to seal, and plastic wrap is useful if the product is cold when sealed.

The best vinegar should be used for pickling, and it should have an acetic acid content of at least 5%. Distilled vinegar, which is colorless, gives a good appearance, but cider vinegar gives a better flavor to pickles and is excellent for chutneys and fruit pickles, as well as relishes.

There is some difference of opinion as to whether the vinegar is best used hot or cold. Try both methods and decide which is the best. One school of thought says that the vinegar has to be boiled with some herbs, or it becomes sour. Others feel that the vinegar keeps fairly well, whatever is pickled in it. A good rule of thumb is that cold vinegar is best for pickling vegetables which need to be kept crisp; for example, onions and red cabbage. Hot vinegar is better with softer pickles, such as plums and walnuts.

Herb vinegars

These are easy to make and add extra flavor to dressings and marinades. Gather the herbs, preferably just before they flower, but you can use the fresh herbs available in the supermarkets if you do not grow your own.

Floral vinegars

These are made in the same way as the herb variety, and they can be used in fruit salads and cosmetic recipes. Again, fresh flowers from the garden are best; choose from elderflowers, nasturtiums, lavender, clover, rose petals, rosemary flowers, thyme flowers, and sweet violets. Remove the stems and any green or white parts from the petals.

Fruit vinegars

These are mostly made from soft fruits, such as raspberries and blackberries, and were used in folk medicine to ease sore throats in times gone by. Today they make an excellent addition to a plain dessert or other baked goods, and have come back into fashion for dressings and marinades.

OILS

Use a good-quality olive, safflower, or sunflower oil. However, beware of using any oil with a strong flavor. It is much cheaper to make your own flavored oils, and a good range will enhance the flavor of your meat, fish, and vegetable cooking, as well as salad dressings. Basil or garlic oil, for example, will flavor pizzas as well as hot or cold tomato dishes.

To make chili oil, pour oil into a bottle containing dried or fresh chilies. Keep for four weeks.

To make a sweet oil, use almond oil with scented flowers, such as lavender, carnations, rose petals, and lemon verbena.

Herbal Vinegar

Use bay leaves, basil, chervil, dill, fennel, lemon balm, marjoram, mint, rosemary, summer savory, tarragon, or thyme.

MAKES 2½ CUPS

2½ cups cider or white wine vinegar
fresh herbs

Bruise the fresh herbs with the back of a spoon, or a weight covered in plastic wrap. Put into a clean jar.

Heat the vinegar, but do not boil, and pour over the herbs when it is warm. Seal with a vinegar-proof top, and place on a warm sunny windowsill. Lift the bottle or jar and shake every day for at least two weeks.

Strain the vinegar and taste for flavor. If a stronger herb taste is required, put more fresh herbs in the vinegar and repeat the process.

Strain into a clean bottle or jar, and add a sprig of fresh herb for decoration and identification.

Spiced Vinegar

Use whole spices because the ground variety gives a cloudy result.

MAKES 5 CUPS

5 cups cider vinegar
1 cinnamon stick
½ tsp whole cloves
½ tsp whole mace
½ tsp whole allspice

Pour the cold vinegar into a sterilized jar or bottle, and put the spices into the vinegar. Shake well, then seal with a vinegar-proof cap. Keep in a cool place for one or two months, taking the container out and shaking every week.

Strain into a suitable sterilized container, and use as required for pickles and chutneys.

Tarragon Vinegar

MAKES ABOUT 2½ CUPS

freshly gathered tarragon leaves, washed
2½ cups white wine vinegar

Use a widemouthed jar which will hold just over the 2½ cups, or adjust the quantity of vinegar.

Preferably, use the herbs just before the plants flower and half-fill the jar with the leaves; then pour on the vinegar. Put on a vinegar-proof cap or stopper, and shake well. Allow the vinegar to steep for at least two weeks, although five weeks is better.

Use as required, without straining.

Aromatic Rosemary Vinegar

MAKES 2½ CUPS

2½ cups white wine vinegar
several large sprigs of rosemary, washed

Put the cold vinegar in a suitable bottle and insert the branches of the rosemary. Leave the bottle, suitably stoppered, for about four to six weeks before using.

Strain, then put a small sprig of fresh rosemary into the bottle for identification.

Fiery Spiced Vinegar

Use whole spices for this recipe.

MAKES 4 QT

4 qt cider vinegar
1½ cups sugar
3 cloves garlic, lightly crushed
3 tbsp allspice
3 tbsp mace
3 tbsp celery seed
2 tbsp cloves
3 tbsp mustard seed
2 tbsp peppercorns
3 tbsp ginger root
1 tsp coriander seeds

Put all the ingredients in a large pan and bring to a boil slowly. Allow to boil for about 5 minutes, then cover and allow to cool naturally. Pour into containers with the spices, and allow to stand for four weeks. The spices can be strained off or left, as liked.

Mint Vinegar

MAKES 2½ CUPS

2½ cups white wine vinegar
large bunch of mint, washed
1 tsp superfine sugar

Heat the vinegar in a saucepan. Crush half the mint leaves into the pan with the vinegar, add the sugar, and bring the vinegar to a boil. Remove immediately from the heat and allow to become cold.

Place the remaining mint leaves in a bottle, and strain in the cooled vinegar. The vinegar is ready to use, but the flavor will become stronger with time.

Garlic Vinegar

MAKES 2½ CUPS

2½ cups red or white wine vinegar
6 cloves garlic

Put the vinegar into a clean jar or a bottle. Slice 3 cloves of garlic and put into the vinegar. Stopper the top and place on a sunny windowsill for about 14 days.

Shake the bottle daily, then strain into a clean bottle. Add the remaining cloves of garlic, peeled but left whole, put on a lid or vinegar-proof cap or stopper, and use as required.

Chili Vinegar

MAKES 2½ CUPS

2½ cups white wine vinegar
¼ cup dried red chilies

Bring the vinegar to a boil and put in the dried chilies. Pour into a jar or a bottle, and keep for five or six weeks, turning over from time to time. Alternatively, boil up the vinegar and add about 6 fresh chilies, deseeded and cut into halves. Both these vinegars are strong, and you will only need a few drops for seasoning.

Chili Sherry

This makes an excellent flavoring for oriental dishes. Put 6 fresh chilies in a bottle and pour in the sherry. Stopper the bottle and keep for 2 weeks before using. The bottle can be refilled with sherry as it is used.

Sherry Ginger is a successful way to store excess fresh ginger root, because this goes moldy quite quickly in the refrigerator. Peel the ginger, place in a suitable small jar, and cover with sherry. Delicious for flavoring oriental dishes or ginger-flavored desserts.

Raspberry Vinegar

This can also be made with black currants and blackberries.

MAKES 4½ CUPS

1 lb ripe raspberries, hulled and washed
2½ cups malt or white wine vinegar
sugar

Put the raspberries into a bowl with the vinegar and cover with a cloth or plastic wrap. Leave to stand for five days, stirring occasionally.

Strain and measure the liquid into a pan. For each 2½ cups liquid, add 1 lb sugar. Bring to a boil for 10 minutes and bottle.

Fragrant Herbal Oils

Use basil, chervil, dill, fennel, lemon balm, marjoram, mint, rosemary, summer savory, tarragon, thyme, or garlic.

MAKES 2½ CUPS

2½ cups good-quality oil
fresh herbs

Bruise the fresh herbs with the back of a spoon or a weight covered in plastic wrap. Put into a clean jar, and cover with unheated oil. Put on a lid and allow to stand on a sunny windowsill for about two weeks.

Strain the oil through a sieve lined with cheesecloth. If a stronger herb taste is required, use more fresh herbs in the oil and repeat the process.

Strain into a clean bottle or jar, and add a sprig of the fresh herb for decoration and identification.

CHAPTER EIGHT

Home Pickling

~

ALTHOUGH THERE ARE many excellent pickles produced commercially, many more people are now making their own.

Use good-quality young vegetables; wash, and remove outer leaves or any blemishes. These can be soaked in brine or sprinkled with salt in layers, as preferred. To make brine, add 2 cups pickling salt to 5 qt water. Rinse the salt from the vegetables and drain before pickling in the vinegar, or else they will be too salty.

Pack the vegetables in sterilized jars and allow ½ inch of vinegar at the top of the jar. There will be some evaporation, and if the vegetables are left uncovered they will become discolored.

After the vinegar has been poured in the jars, they should be sealed tightly with vinegar-proof tops. Use the metal lids and screw bands that fit canning jars. Otherwise, waxed paper tied with string is suitable, or use plastic wrap for sealing cold pickles.

Garlicky Pickled Cucumbers

MAKES 4½ CUPS

2¼ lb small cucumbers
(3–5 inches long)
1 cup pickling salt
10 cups water
Spiced Vinegar (*see* page 68)
2 cloves garlic, peeled and sliced

Scrub the cucumbers, rinse well, and lay them in a glass or china bowl. Pour on the salt, then the water, and stir around. Cover with plastic wrap and leave for three days.

Slice the cucumbers into rings, and pack into sterilized jars.

Heat the spiced vinegar with the garlic, and pour over the cucumbers. Cover with plastic wrap and leave for 24 hours in a warm kitchen or cupboard.

Drain off the vinegar and boil up again (you may need to add more). Pour over the cucumbers, and leave for another 24 hours. Repeat the process until the cucumbers have become darker.

Seal with vinegar-proof lids, and allow to stand for at least one week before using.

If liked, put a sprig of dill and some dill flowers in each jar in the final stage before storing.

Red Cabbage Relish

MAKES ABOUT 8 CUPS

1 red cabbage
Pickling salt
Spiced Vinegar (*see* page 68)

Remove any discolored leaves from the outside of the cabbage and shred finely (this can be done in the food processor). Arrange a layer of cabbage and sprinkle with salt. Continue with other layers of cabbage and salt until the final layer is salted. Allow to stand for 24 hours.

Wash and rinse the cabbage to remove excess salt. Pack into jars (the amount will depend on the size of the cabbage) and cover with spiced vinegar. Eat after three or four days for a crisp relish. Although the cabbage will keep for several months, it will become soft after about 2 months.

Pickled Walnuts

The walnuts must be picked before they become woody and develop a shell. They can be tested by pricking with a needle; if any shell is felt, the nut should be discarded for this purpose. Beware of the stain; it is better to use disposable rubber gloves for this task.

MAKES QUANTITY OF NUTS PREPARED

English walnuts, as available
2 cups salt
5 qt water
7½ cups malt or cider vinegar
2⅔ cups dark brown sugar
1½ tsp salt
1 tsp whole mixed spice
1 tsp black peppercorns
½ tsp cloves

Make up half the salt and water, and pour over the nuts in a glass or china bowl. Leave for three or four days. Drain the nuts, and steep in the remaining half of the brine solution for one week.

Drain the nuts and arrange on plastic trays or china dishes. Leave the nuts for about one day, until they have turned completely black. Put the remaining ingredients in a saucepan and dissolve the sugar slowly. Bring to a boil for about 5 minutes. Allow to cool for several hours, then strain out the spices.

Arrange the walnuts in jars, then heat up the strained vinegar and pour onto the walnuts. Cover the jars with vinegar-proof lids, and allow to stand for at least four weeks before opening.

Pickled Horseradish

MAKES 1 CUP

Horseradish roots, washed and grated
½ tsp sugar for each jar
½ tsp salt for each jar
1 fresh chili, sliced (optional)
distilled white vinegar

Fill small sterilized jars two-thirds full with grated horseradish. Add sugar and salt to each jar with a slice of chili. Cover with vinegar and seal well for storage.

Use the horseradish as a condiment for beef or smoked fish, and for sprinkling on cooked red beets.

Pickled Onions

MAKES 8 CUPS

4 lb pickling onions
2 cups salt
5 qt water
Spiced Vinegar (see page 68)

Use small, even-sized onions, and put them in a large bowl or pot with the skins on. Make up half the salt and water into a brine, and pour over the onions. Leave the onions for 12 hours, then drain, peel, and return to the bowl. Make up the other half of the brine, and pour over the peeled onions. Allow to stand for at least 36 hours. Use a plate or lid to keep the onions under the brine.

Drain the onions in a plastic colander or strain thoroughly, and then pack into sterilized jars. Pour on the cold spiced vinegar, seal, and store for at least three or four months before using.

Pickled Mushrooms

MAKES 2 CUPS

1 lb button mushrooms, washed
2½ cups Spiced Vinegar (see page 68)
2 blades mace
½ tsp white pepper
1 tsp salt
1 tsp ground ginger
½ onion

Put the mushrooms in a pan with 1¼ cups vinegar, add the other ingredients, and cook on a low heat until the mushrooms become smaller and cooked. Strain the mushrooms and pack into sterilized jars.

Add the remaining 1¼ cups vinegar to the pan and reheat. When hot, pour onto the mushrooms. Seal and cover.

Pickled Green Tomato

MAKES ABOUT 6 CUPS

3 lb green tomatoes, washed
salt
1¼ cups vinegar
1 tsp cinnamon

Use 1 tbsp salt to 4½ cups water, and boil the tomatoes for about 10 minutes. Lift out with a fork and peel off the skin. Boil the vinegar, cinnamon, and ⅔ cup water together, add the tomatoes, and boil for 5 minutes. Pour into a plastic or glass bowl, cover with plastic wrap, and allow to stand for a week.

Strain off the vinegar and boil in a pan for 10 minutes. Add the tomatoes and cook for 5 minutes. Pack into sterilized jars and seal while hot.

Spiced Mixed Vegetable Relish

MAKES ABOUT 8 CUPS

1 cauliflower, cut into small florets
1 lb pickling onions,
peeled and halved
3 cups trimmed and sliced green beans
2 cucumbers, washed and sliced
1 cup salt
10 cups water
Spiced Vinegar (see page 68)

Prepare the vegetables, and put into a large glass or china bowl. Sprinkle over the salt and pour on the water. Mix well, cover with plastic wrap, and leave to stand for at least 48 hours.

Wash and drain the vegetables, and pack into jars, leaving some space for the vinegar to surround the vegetables. Cover with the cold spiced vinegar and seal with vinegar-proof lids. Allow to stand for at least two weeks before using.

Spicy Piccalilli

There are two main types of piccalilli, the spicy variety and the sweeter relish.

MAKES 6 PT

2 cups salt
5 qt water
6 lb mixed fresh vegetables
(cauliflower florets, pickling onions or
shallots, green beans, zucchini, strips of
bell pepper, diced cucumber)
2 tbsp turmeric
5 tbsp powdered mustard
5 tbsp ground ginger
¾ cup sugar
1 tbsp cornstarch
5 cups distilled white vinegar

Make up the salt and water in a large bowl. As the vegetables are prepared, drop them into the brine. Cover with a heavy lid, plate, or board to keep the vegetables immersed in the brine. Allow the vegetables to soak in the brine for 24 hours, before rinsing in cold water and draining.

Measure the spices with the sugar into a large pan. Add three-quarters of the vinegar, and stir on a low heat until well mixed and the sugar is dissolved.

Add the prepared vegetables, and stir until well coated with the spice mixture and the vegetables are slightly tender. However, they are better crisp (not hard) and should not be overcooked.

Lift the vegetables out with a slotted spoon and pack into sterilized jars, allowing enough space for the sauce.

Mix the cornstarch with the remaining vinegar, and mix into the liquid in the pan. Boil for a few minutes. Pour the sauce into the jars, turning around to allow it to coat the vegetables. Alternatively, you can thicken the sauce while the vegetables are still in the pan, making sure that no lumps form, and then pack into jars.

Sweet Piccalilli

MAKES 6 PT

2 cups salt
5 qt water
6 lb mixed fresh vegetables
(cauliflower florets, pickling onions or
shallots, green beans, zucchini, strips of
bell pepper, diced cucumber, green
tomatoes and sliced celery)
2 tbsp turmeric
3 tbsp powdered mustard
1½ tsp ground ginger
1 cup sugar
2 tbsp cornstarch
7½ cups distilled white vinegar

Make up the salt and water in a large bowl. As the vegetables are prepared, drop them into the brine. Cover with a heavy lid, plate, or board to keep the vegetables immersed in the brine. Allow the vegetables to soak in the brine for 24 hours, before rinsing in cold water and draining.

Measure the spices with the sugar into a large pan. Add three-quarters of the vinegar and stir around over a low heat, until well mixed and the sugar is dissolved.

Add the prepared vegetables, and stir until well coated with the spice mixture and the vegetables are slightly tender. However, they are better crisp (not hard) and on no account should be overcooked until soft and mushy.

Lift the vegetables out with a slotted spoon and pack into sterilized jars, allowing enough space for the sauce to go around them.

Mix the cornstarch with the remaining vinegar, and mix into the liquid in the pan. Boil for a few minutes. Pour the sauce into the jars, turning around to allow it to coat the vegetables.

CHAPTER NINE

Crystallized, Candied, and Glacé Fruits

~

THESE ARE EXPENSIVE to buy and often imported from France. The fruits take a long time to prepare, but it is easy and much cheaper to prepare candied fruits at home, if you have the time and patience. The process consists of covering the fruit at first with a light, hot syrup, made with granulated sugar, and then continuing the process over several days with increased sugar syrup, until the fruit is totally impregnated with sugar. The fruit is often finished by crystallizing, which gives it a sugary appearance, or by glazing in a syrup, which gives a glacé finish.

SUITABLE FRUIT AND PEEL

Apricots, cherries, pineapples, plums, peaches, and grapes are all suitable. Peel of citrus fruits and angelica can also be treated, but flower petals and herb leaves need a different process (see later).

It is best to candy each fruit separately to retain the individual flavors. Small fruits, such as cherries and apricots, should be pitted, and larger fruits peeled and halved. Fruit should be fresh and firm. Soft fruits, such as raspberries and strawberries, are not suitable.

CANDIED FRUIT

This process can take two weeks for larger pieces of fruit.

Preparation

Whole fruit should be pricked by a fork (all old cookbooks stipulate a silver fork, but a stainless steel one will serve); larger fruits can be halved or quartered.

Prepare the fruit, and then weigh it before putting it in a large saucepan. Cover with hot water and simmer until just soft, but not overcooked or mushy. Reserve the cooking liquid, and transfer the fruit into a large heatproof bowl large enough to keep the fruit covered.

For every 1 lb prepared fruit, a syrup will be needed, which can be made up with the cooking liquid to 1¼ cups. To the water, add ¼ cup sugar and ½ cup glucose (all sugar can be used, but this mixture is better). Bring the sugar and water slowly to a boil to allow the sugar to dissolve, and continue boiling until you have a thin syrup. If there is not enough, make more because the fruit must be covered.

Method

1 Pour the hot syrup over the fruit until completely covered. Place plastic wrap over the top of the bowl, and leave for 24 hours.

2 Drain off the syrup into a saucepan and add ¼ cup sugar. Bring to a boil, and pour over the fruit again. Repeat this process of adding the extra sugar, boiling the syrup, and pouring over the fruit for four more days.

3 On the fifth day, drain off the syrup into a saucepan and add ⅓ cup sugar or glucose to the syrup. Add the fruit from the bowl and boil for 3 minutes. Return the fruit and syrup to the bowl, and allow to stand, covered, for 48 hours.

4 Repeat stage 3, and then leave the fruit to soak for four days. By now the syrup should be very thick, almost like honey. If the syrup is not as thick as this, repeat stage 3 again.

Drying

Arrange a fine-meshed wire rack over a clean plastic tray or dish, and lift the fruit from the syrup with a slotted spoon onto the wire rack. After it has dripped, it can be left to dry in a warm cupboard or kitchen. The temperature should not be more than 120°F. If the temperature is steady, the fruits will dry out in a few hours; otherwise it might take some days. Turn the fruit from time to time until it is completely dry, and then it is ready to use.

CRYSTALLIZED FRUIT

To finish the fruit in this way, have ready a layer of granulated sugar on paper laid out on a tray. Dip each fruit into boiling water and drain off excess moisture. Roll each fruit in the sugar until coated, and allow to dry.

GLACE FRUITS

Make these in a warm, dry atmosphere, or the fruits may remain sticky.

1 Make a new syrup of 2 cups sugar slowly dissolved in ⅔ cup water, then brought to a boil. Keep the syrup in a tightly covered dish.

2 Heat a dish or cup by pouring boiling water onto it, and then emptying. Pour a small amount of syrup into the warm dish or cup.

3 Dip the candied fruit in boiling water and drain. Dip into the syrup in the cup, and arrange on a wire rack. When the syrup in the cup becomes cloudy, discard the syrup and replace with more.

4 When all the fruits are arranged on the wire rack, allow to dry in a warm, dry atmosphere, turning over from time to time.

Marrons Glacés

These are not the same as the commercially prepared chestnuts from France because it is impossible to produce those at home. However, these are delicious and worth doing when chestnuts are in season.

2¼ lb chestnuts
2 cups sugar
2 cups glucose
1¼ cups water (for syrup)
vanilla extract

Remove the shells by making a slit at the pointed end of each nut with a sharp knife. Place them in a large saucepan and cover with cold water. Bring the water slowly to a boil and cook for 2 minutes. Remove from the water with a slotted spoon, and take off the shells when cool enough to handle (use rubber gloves).

To prepare in the microwave, make the slits at the ends and microwave on high for 3 minutes for each 8 oz. Turn the chestnuts after 2 minutes, then remove and peel.

Put the peeled chestnuts into a pan, cover with cold water, bring gently to a boil, and simmer until tender. Drain carefully to avoid breaking.

While the chestnuts are cooking, make a syrup in a large pan by mixing the sugar and glucose with the water over a low heat, and stir until the sugar is dissolved. Bring to a boil for about 4 minutes, then add the chestnuts and gently bring the pan back to a boil. Cover the pan, and allow to stand overnight in a warm place.

Bring the saucepan back to a boil, cover, and allow to stand for a further 24 hours. Add a few drops of vanilla extract and slowly bring to a boil again.

Allow the syrup to cool slightly, then remove the chestnuts from the syrup and drain on a wire cooling rack, placed over a tray to catch the drips. Use the glacé method to finish.

Candied Angelica

Use the stalks of the plant when young and tender, which means cutting them in April or May. Trim off the roots and leaf end, and place the stalks in a bowl.

Make a brine by putting 2 tbsp salt into 5 cups water. Bring to a boil and pour over the stalks. Allow to soak for about 10 minutes. Drain and rinse in cold water, then put in a saucepan of boiling water. Boil for 5 minutes, or longer if the stalks seem tough. Scrape the stalks to remove the outer skin.

Make a syrup of 1 cup sugar and 1 cup glucose dissolved slowly in 2½ cups water. Boil until the liquid becomes slightly thicker.

Arrange the angelica in a long plastic container. Pour the syrup on top of the angelica and leave for about two weeks, refilling with glucose every second day until the syrup is thick.

Candied Peel

Prepare the peels of oranges, grapefruit, and lemons by scrubbing the peels thoroughly. Cut in half, and remove the juice and pulp.

Boil the peels for about 1 hour, changing the water several times. Drain and follow the procedure for angelica, allowing the peel to soak for three weeks. Finish as for Glacé Fruits.

Use the leftover syrup for fruit salads or stewing fruits, or dilute and use for any further candying process again.

Crystallized Flowers

These can be made at home, and make lovely decorations for cakes and desserts.

Use almost any flower, except those grown from bulbs (they are poisonous) or indeed any poisonous plants. Small flowers, such as violets, primroses, and cherry blossoms, are most suitable. Pick on a dry day, without rain or dew on the petals.

Gum arabic and rose water are both available from gourmet cooking stores.

Method 1

Pour 2 tbsp rose water into a screw-top jar with ½ oz gum arabic. Shake well and put to one side for several hours, shaking the jar every 30 minutes.

Line a baking sheet with parchment paper. Cut the stalks from the flowers, or leave small stalks if using tiny sprigs. Individual petals can also be removed from the flower heads.

Use a small, soft paintbrush, and brush both sides of the flowers with the gum arabic mixture. Dip the flowers into superfine sugar and place on the baking sheet. Leave in a warm place to dry. Store in a glass jar with an airtight lid.

Method 2

Make a syrup using 2 cups sugar and 1 cup water. Simmer until the sugar is dissolved, and then boil for about 5–7 minutes.

Drop the petals or flower heads into the syrup and boil for 1 minute. Remove from the syrup with a slotted spoon, drain, and arrange on a tray lined with waxed paper. Use tweezers to arrange the petals, if necessary.

Leave in a warm place for 24 hours to dry. Store in an airtight glass jar.

Index